Topographical Map of Black Rock Region

From U.S. Geological Survey
Map of Nevada

10   0   10 Miles

THE
BLACK ROCK
DESERT

OTHER BOOKS BY SESSIONS S. WHEELER

Paiute
The Desert Lake, The Story of Nevada's Pyramid Lake
The Nevada Desert

NEVADA'S BLACK ROCK DESERT

By

SESSIONS S. WHEELER

and Illustrated By

Nevada's Desert Artist

J. Craig Sheppard

CAXTON PRESS

Caldwell, Idaho 83605

2003

First printing May, 1978
Second printing October, 1979
Third printing January, 1985
Fourth printing December, 1994
Fifth printing September, 2003

Library of Congress Cataloging in Publication Data

Wheeler, Sessions S
    The Black Rock desert.

    Includes bibliographical references.
    1. Black Rock Desert, Nev. — History. I. Title.
F847.B53W47   979.3′54   76-6648
ISBN 0-87004-258-0

Lihographed and bound in the United States of America by
Caxton Press
Caldwell, Idaho 83605
170084

To Black Rock
Desert Companions
Harold, Jim and Virginia
Clayton and Virginia
Thayer and Marjorie
Bill and Rudy
Scoop and Inez
Ken and Vince
And, of course,
Craig, Yo and Nevada

Acknowledgment

I HOPE the following people realize my gratitude for the help they provided:

Clara Robison, secretarial aid; Mike Conway, photography; Ralph Parman, information; Mrs. Verne Parman, information; Dr. Vincent Gianella, information and technical review; Ken Carpenter, critical review; Don Tuohy, archeology information; Mary Date, secretarial; Mary Neff, secretarial; Tom Trelease, information; Mitchell Bidart, information; Clyde Fisk, information; Mark and Elsie Anderson, photographs; Dr. Robert Amesbury, photographs; Mrs. Elizabeth Hallum, Lassen County librarian, review; Thomas C. Wilson, information; Mr. Chester Conrad, Bureau of Land Management, information; Harry Drackert, information; Fred Parrish, information; Louis Lay, information; Laurance Fee, review; Dr. James Herz; Catherine Jensen, research.

General aid from libraries include University of Nevada Library, Special Collections; Washoe County Library Reference Desk; California State Library; Humboldt County Library; Nevada Historical Society; National Archives; Department of Army, Center of Military history; University of California Bancroft Library.

For their interest and help in many ways, my thanks to Sol and Ella Savitt.

Table of Contents

Chapter		Page
I.	BEFORE IT WAS DESERT	19
II.	THE DESERT'S NATURE	35
III.	ITS FIRST NON-INDIANS	40
IV.	THE DEATH ROUTE	49
V.	THE DESERT'S INDIAN WAR	78
VI.	THE LOST SILVER LODE AND THE ROCK HOUNDS	137
VII.	THE RANCHERS	151
VIII.	THE DESERT TODAY	172
	APPENDIX	189

List of Illustrations

The Famous Black Rock . . . . Frontispiece

Page

Light reflecting from the playa surface 21
Terraces formed by ancient Lake Lahontan 23
Lake Lahontan covered more than 8,000 square miles . 25
Dry lake bed was once submerged beneath water 27
Mysterious crescents were made out of rock 28
Artifacts were found on surface of Black Rock playa . . . 31
"Last Supper Cave" 33
King Lear Peak of the Jackson Range 37
High Rock Canyon 41
Smoke indicated hot springs 43
Applegate brothers gave the Black Rock its name 51
Peter Lassen, famous California pioneer 53
Lassen's Route 55
Ox shoe on the emigrant trail 57
Craig makes sketch for painting 59
From a rise they could see Black Rock 61
Thousands of travelers passed over this road 63
Old trail heads for the Black Rock 65
Hot spring first goal of travelers 66
Hillocks of dry mud seperate the playa 67
High Rock Canyon 69
Wagon ruts in High Rock Canyon 69
Rabbit Hole Springs unpleasant for late arrivals 70
High Rock Canyon has changed very little 71
Barren flat they must cross 73
Lunch stop with "Fremont's Castle" in background 75
Field trip of the Trails West organization 76

Page

Clapper's grave? 85
Colonel Charles McDermit and his family 89
Fort Churchill on the Carson River 91
T-bar posts made of railroad rails 93
Famed Nevada race horse, Washoe Queen 99
Last page of Captain Wells' official report 103
Remains of the Granite Creek Station 109
Band of the Third Infantry, California Volunteers 111
E. D. Pierce operated stage line 113
Denio to Winnemucca freight team, 1868 115
Dun Glen was a mining camp 117
Natural fortress in Paiute Creek canyon 119
From above the Paiute canyon fortress 121
Paiute Creek canyon excellent terrain for ambush 122
The morning being very cold and stormy 126
The men ran in circles to keep warm 129
A dense cloud of frost commenced flying 131
Battle Creek 134
Erosion has almost eradicated Hardin City 140
Enroute to Hardin City 141
A Varyville residence 143
In June snow can still be seen 145
Rockhounds like to camp at Double Hot Springs 147
Half of geode from Black Rock Desert basin 148
Areas provide grazing for cattle and sheep 152
George Parman in early nineteen-twenties 153
Cabin at Summit Lake built about 1884 154
The Parman brothers 155
Miller and Lux freight team, 1885 157
Miller Lux, 1898 158
Denio wool freight teams, 1885 159
Deep Hole Ranch, 1890s 160
Deep Hole Ranch, 1890s 161
Few charred boards of ranch house remain 161

Page

Painting of typical sheepherder's camp 165
Summer sheep camp on Summit Lake mountain 167
Corral at Leonard Creek Ranch 168
Charlie and Hattie Painter 169
Town of Gerlach probably in mid 1920s 173
Bruno Selmi on Gerlach's main street 173
Thunderhead building over the desert 177
Many people visit the hot springs 178
A desert camp and Jackson Mountains 180
Rain clouds warn it is time to leave 181
Black Rock photographed from aircraft 185

Maps

Topographical Map of Black Rock
    Region .... Inside Front Cover

Note to the Reader

CRAIG AND I love the desert. For many years we have traveled the Black Rock until now there are not many square miles of the ancient lake bed unknown to us.

Craig is able to express his feelings for the desert in his paintings. I am limited to written words, which often are difficult to find when I know they will be read by some people who have never experienced the type of beauty, the freedom, and the solitude the great desert offers.

We are both history buffs, and one purpose of this book is the same as that of my other Nevada books — to gather the interesting history of a region and make it more readily available to readers who enjoy western Americana.

And we have an additional incentive, the hope that more widespread knowledge of the beauty and history of this unusual part of the earth may help to save it from destruction — at least from anything like the once-proposed degradation of becoming San Francisco's giant garbage dump.

SSW

THE
BLACK ROCK
DESERT

TO SOME it seems hostile and frightening, its past known for violence and hardship. To others it is a bright and friendly part of this earth, a place where men have found adventure.

It is spectacular and strange, a vast barren plain which, though enclosed and shaped by rugged mountains, stretches for more than one hundred miles in a southwest-to-northeast direction. Geographers consider it a playa, the dry bed of an ancient lake lying within the large Great Basin Desert. But a modern dictionary gives it individual status by listing it, along with the Sahara, as one of the forty-seven major deserts of the world.

At one place jutting mountains pinch its width to a narrow corridor so that early pioneers considered it two deserts. The smaller southern section took the name of a stream, Smoke Creek, which periodically flows to the playa's edge. The northern section is named for a dark rock hill, approximately four hundred feet high, which in the early days provided a travelers' landmark. At a distance, contrasted with the lighter background of its mountain range, it resembles a massive black rock.

CHAPTER I

Before It Was Desert

H E WAS OLD, and he welcomed the morning sun which now warmed his back and brightened the colors of the mountains across the valley. From this foothill above the edge of the marsh he could follow the fishing activities of his people while his hands were busy chipping a piece of stone with a tool made of deer antler. Small flakes glittered as they fell, and now the rock was becoming pointed, its edges sharp. Soon it would be ready to replace a spearpoint which water-softened bindings had left buried in mud.

Beyond the green of the marshland, a shallow lake stretched to the south and west. Watching it, he thought again about the mystery of the scars on the mountains. For as long as anyone could remember, his people had come here during the seasons when the fish were easy to catch and the water birds, discarding worn wing feathers, were unable to fly. During his own lifetime the lake had varied in depth many times, and he had understood these changes because they corresponded to the amounts of rain and snow provided by winter skies. He remembered one long period when streams had run bank full, and the lake had crept up to the base of the foothills. Below him he could still see the scar made by its waves.

But here, and throughout the country of his

people, there were similar scars high on the mountainsides. Years ago he and his eldest grandson had examined one of the terraces and, amazingly, had found stone knives and other rock implements which were so waterworn their chipped surfaces were almost smooth.

At that time there had been other, more practical, problems to think about; but during the last few years, since his skill with a chipping tool had become his only asset to his band, there had been ample opportunity to wonder whether the lines on the mountains could have been made by waves and to recall the old legends which claimed that other humans had lived in this land long before his people came here. Was it possible they had hunted and fished along the shores of a lake so deep and so large that it stretched over much of the country his band now roamed?

He had discussed it with his grandson last evening, and although the younger man had, as always, listened intently, there had been doubt in his eyes.

Now, as the old man worked a final side groove into the base of the spearpoint, he wished there was a way to test his theory, perhaps to follow the scars to determine whether they continued along the sides of other mountains and eventually returned here. He was unable to travel that far, and he doubted that anyone else would ever seek the answer to his question.

Early explorers and other nineteenth century travelers crossing the valleys which are now part of

LIGHT REFLECTING FROM THE PLAYA SURFACE GIVES THE BLACK ROCK DESERT THE APPEARANCE OF THE LAKE IT WAS THOUSANDS OF YEARS AGO.

northwestern Nevada noted the tufa and other in-
dications of an ancient lake. In 1867 famed
geologist Clarence King mapped a portion of the
area and named it for explorer Baron de
Lahontan.[1] But it was not until April of 1881 that
a systematic study of the prehistoric lake bed was
begun.

Israel C. Russell, a geologist with the U.S.
Geological Survey and a former professor at Columbia University, was described as "slightly below
medium height, and of rather slender frame, so
that he seemed frail, but really possessed great
strength, agility, and endurance."[2] The official report of his geological reconnaissance travels in the
Great Basin leaves little doubt that he felt at ease
in a wilderness environment.

Russell's first year of exploration of Lake
Lahontan was planned as a preliminary investigation without scientific assistants or detailed studies.
Working alone during seven months of 1881, Russell traveled on horseback the considerable distance of 3,500 miles on a route which crossed and
recrossed the Lahontan Basin and took him into
some of the most primitive areas of the West. Even
with today's off-road vehicles and modern camping equipment it would be a rugged journey, but
his report gives no attention to the hardships, tel-
ling instead of the beauty and solitude that he
found. With realism he wrote, "The scenery on
the larger playas is peculiar, and usually desolate
in the extreme, but yet is not without its charms.
In crossing these wastes the traveler may ride for
miles over a perfectly level floor, with an un-

Courtesy Nevada State Museum
TERRACES FORMED BY ANCIENT LAKE LAHONTAN CAN BE
SEEN HIGH ABOVE THE DRY LAKE BED.

broken skyline before him and not an object in
sight to cast a shadow on the oceanlike expanse.
Mirages may be seen every day on these heated
deserts. Similar optical illusions give strange, fan-
ciful forms to the mountains, and sometimes
transfigure them beyond all recognition. At such
times a packtrain crossing the desert a few miles
distant frequently appears like some strange cara-
van of grotesque beasts fording a shallow lake, the
shores of which advance as one rides away. The
monotony of midday on the desert is thus broken

by delusive forms that are ever changing and suggest a thousand fancies which divert the attention from the fatigues of the journey. The cool evenings and mornings in these arid regions, when the purple shadows of distant mountains are thrown across the plain, have a charm that is unknown beneath more humid skies. The profound stillness of the night in these solitudes is always impressive."[3]

During the 1882 and 1883 field seasons detailed geologic studies were completed, and in 1885 the U.S. Geological Survey published Russell's monograph, *Geological History of Lake Lahontan, a Quarternary Lake of Northwestern Nevada*. This large book has been the starting place for most of the later studies of the prehistory of the region.

Geologists agree that the valleys which formed the long, irregularly shaped Lake Lahontan began to fill with water approximately seventy thousand years ago during a prehistoric time period called the Pleistocene epoch. During the following sixty thousand years, while the last great ice sheet from the north crept down and then retreated from what is now north-central and northeastern United States, the climate changed many times. When the weather was cooler and wetter, relatively small glaciers formed in the Sierra Nevada and other mountains of the West, and Lake Lahontan responded by increasing in depth and surface area so that several times it covered more than eight thousand square miles.

A current U.S. Geological Survey map of the Black Rock Desert shows an elevation of 3,848 feet

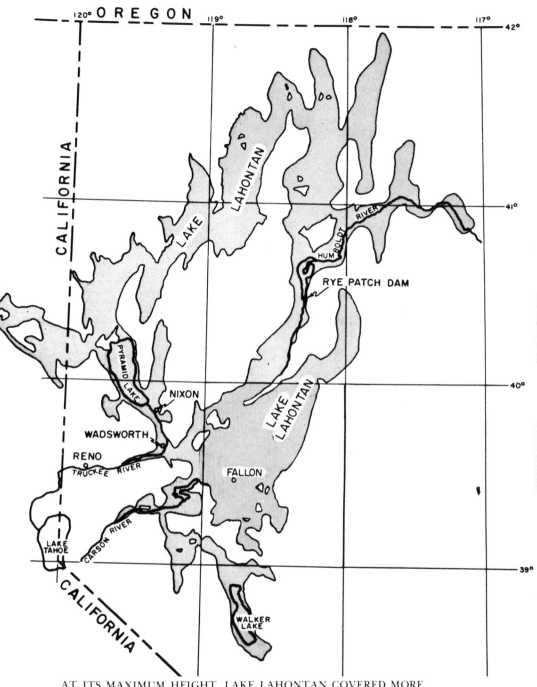

AT ITS MAXIMUM HEIGHT, LAKE LAHONTAN COVERED MORE
THAN 8,000 SQUARE MILES.

above sea level for the sink of the Queen's (Quinn) River. Comparing this figure with Lahontan's approximate maximum surface elevation of 4,380 feet[4] establishes a difference of 532 feet. While crossing this section of the playa today, it is difficult to visualize that the cementlike surface on which you are riding or walking was once submerged beneath more than 500 feet of water.

During warmer and drier times the big lake retreated from its high-water shores, and there is evidence that it may have dried up completely over at least one long period. It is thought that during most of the past eight to nine thousand years the water in the Lahontan Basin has remained at relatively low levels.

No one knows for certain when man first came to the Black Rock-Smoke Creek region, but carbon dating of organic materials preserved in the dry dust of caves provides strong evidence that he lived in northwestern Nevada at least eleven thousand years ago. Science believes that men of his race had come down from the north, hardy Asian hunters-explorers whose ancestors had crossed the Bering Strait over a temporary land bridge or on winter ice or skin boats to the shores of a new continent. From there, through the centuries, they moved south — some to settle along the way but others, the adventurers, always moving on until they could go no farther by land. They did this not only for food and other necessities but because they were humans — men with the same relentless instincts which drove an Englishman across Africa, a Norwegian to the earth's

IT MAY SEEM DIFFICULT TO VISUALIZE THAT TODAY'S DRY
LAKE BED WAS ONCE SUBMERGED BENEATH 500 FEET OF
WATER.

South Pole, an American into space. The Asian-
Americans explored and spread throughout the
new continents, urged on by an inner force which
demanded to know what was beyond the next valley, the next mountain, the distant horizon.

C. William Clewlow, Jr.[5] suggests a date of 9,700
years before the present as a logical time for man
to have first occupied the Black Rock Desert area,
basing his opinion partially on the decreasing
depth of Lake Lahontan during the last ten
thousand years. Using Morrison's Lahontan geology studies, Clewlow points out that a lake with
an altitude of 3,900 feet or less "would have

created the vast, marshy, lakeside situation into which the present interpretation of the artifact record best fits."

Such an environment would have provided a satisfactory food supply — cutthroat trout and other native fish from the open lake, and waterfowl and other birds and animals from the marshlands. It is easy to imagine ancient hunters and fishermen stalking ducks and geese, especially during the molting season, and catching fish with plant fiber nets or spears. And in certain areas they left behind their projectile points and other artifacts, some of which offer archeologists fascinating puzzles.

Courtesy Mr. and Mrs. Mark Anderson

WHETHER THEY WERE SCRAPERS, FISH GORGES, CHARM STONES, OR TRANSVERSE PROJECTILE POINTS, THE MYSTERIOUS CRESCENTS WERE OFTEN MADE OUT OF BEAUTIFULLY COLORED ROCK.

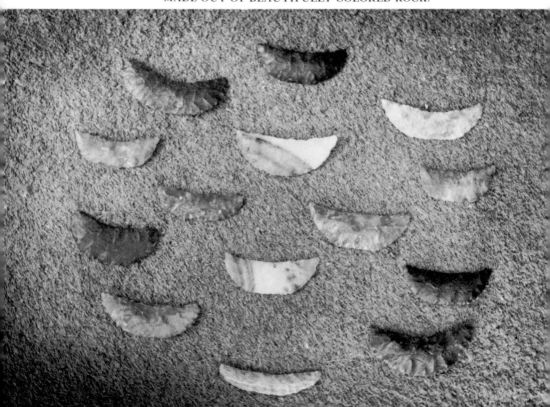

Nevada State Museum archeologist Donald
Tuohy[6] points out that "a group of
quarry–workshops have been located on and
above the 4,380-foot level. Along beach terraces,
formed at lower elevations by waves of the ancient
lake, stone tools have been found, and on the bed
of the playa, projectile points, other artifacts, and
waste flakes have been collected. One small section
of the Black Rock Desert is especially known for its
mysterious "crescents," lunate-shaped objects
often expertly chipped from beautifully colored
rocks. The number of these artifacts found in this
limited area is many times the total collected in the
remainder of the western United States.*

When a crescent is examined, its use invariably
becomes a subject of speculation, with both
amateurs and professionals offering suggestions
which range all the way from fish gorges, scrapers,
charm stones, ceremonial ornaments, or spear
barbs to surgical instruments. Regarding the latter
possibility, Dr. Clewlow commented, "Unless we
imagine a vast pre-Columbian medical center on
the shores of the Black Rock Desert post-Lahontan
lakes, it is difficult to accept the . . . [crescents] as
surgical instruments."

The possibility that the crescents may have been
hafted and used as transverse projectile points for

Author's note: Artifact collectors unfamiliar with the Black Rock Desert
should not conclude that crescents or other types of artifacts are still abun-
dant there. Only relatively small areas of the desert show any indication of
occupation or use by early man, and these have been heavily combed by
many amateur collectors and some professional archeologists so that currently they are far from productive.

Before collecting artifacts on public lands, information on current regula-
tions should be obtained.

stunning birds and other small animals was discussed by Clewlow. "It does not seem unlikely that
stunning points would have been known to hunters of 7,000 to 5,000 B.C. in the Great Basin, and
it is here suggested that the crescentic stone objects under discussion served precisely this purpose. The wide arc or striking surface of a transverse point would provide a greater relative mar-
gin of permitted inaccuracy in firing at small
game. It is a fact well known to modern or-
nithologists (and we can assume the same to have
been true of aboriginal hunters) that birds are easily disabled by the shock of being struck. Unlike
many, perhaps most, other animals, the bird's
physiological reaction to a blow is to immobilize it.
Other animals are less prone to being disabled by
a relatively light shock, and the easiest way to secure them is by more direct means such as pierc-
ing their bodies with a pointed projectile (dart or
arrow). The extensive use of the sling or other
pellet-propulsion devices for bird hunting is
another illustration of the particular susceptibility
of avian forms to disablement by a body blow.
That primitive hunters are capable of recognizing
specific vulnerabilities of certain animals is abun-
dantly proved. . . .

"The limited localities where these crescents are
concentrated at the Black Rock Desert sites represent, in all probability, favored hunting areas for
waterfowl, and the large numbers of crescents at
these spots represent the remains of projectiles
that were fired and not recovered."

However, to add to the mystery, archeologist

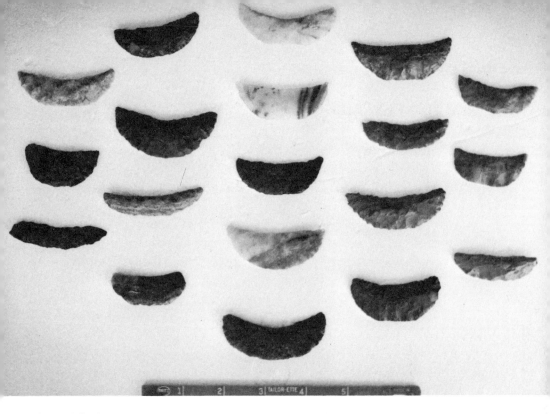

YEARS AGO, CRESCENTS, PROJECTILE POINTS AND OTHER ARTIFACTS WERE
FOUND ON THE SURFACE OF CERTAIN AREAS OF THE BLACK ROCK PLAYA.
Presently they are scarce.

Donald Tuohy of the Nevada State Museum has a
crescent with a sinew binding around one end,
seeming to indicate that it was not transversely
hafted. Examination revealed that human hairs
were caught up in the binding, which might suggest that it was used as an ornament or ceremonial
object. The crescent was excavated from the dry
dust of a cave on the south side of a mountain
ridge bordering the Black Rock Desert.

Some archeologists have tentatively dated the
crescent artifacts at approximately 5,000 to 7,000
B.C. Were the people who made them the
forefathers of the Indians who occupied northern
Nevada at the time of the first white explorers?

No, answer anthropologists, except in a sense
that all American Indians originally came from
Asia. When the white man first arrived, the region
now known as northwestern Nevada was occupied
by the Northern Paiute people. Cave excavations
have provided evidence that these Indians did not
come to this section of the Great Basin until approximately 1,400 A.D. and that at least three
other separate cultures of people preceded them.
It seems certain that one of the earlier cultures —
thousands of years earlier — manufactured the
crescents, probably during one or more of the
periods when Lake Lahontan's surface elevation
created marshlands.

It would seem logical that desiccation of the
Lake and marshes into a dry playa would have
ended the Indian's occupation of the area; but the
observations of explorer John Charles Fremont,
Lassen Trail emigrants, and the military show that

NEVADA STATE MUSEUM OFFICIALS AND GUESTS VISITED THE "LAST SUPPER
CAVE" EXCAVATION NORTH OF THE BLACK ROCK DESERT, IN 1973.
Radiocarbon dating indicated human occupation more than 9,000 years ago.

the Paiute and other tribes used it long after it became barren desert.

Actually, as will be told in a later chapter, it was
one of the Indian warriors' last refuges.

NOTES TO CHAPTER I

1. Louis Armand de Lom d'Arce, Baron de Lahontan, a Frenchman, in
1688 traveled to the Mississippi River where he discovered a stream which
flowed to the west. He claimed to have followed this stream to its headwat-

ers, where Indians told him of another stream flowing west which emptied into a salt lake, which in turn drained into the ocean.

2. C. A. Davis, "Israel Cook Russell," *Michigan Acad. Sci.,* Rep. 9 (1907), pp. 28–31.

3. Israel C. Russell, *Geologic History of Lake Lahontan, a Quarternary Lake of Northwestern Nevada*, U.S. Geological Survey, Monograph 11 (Washington, D.C., 1885), 288 p.

4. R. B. Morrison, *Lake Lahontan: Geology of the Southern Carson Desert, Nevada*, U.S. Geological Survey, Professional Paper 401 (Washington, D.C., 1964).

5. C. William Clewlow, Jr., *Surface Archeology in the Black Rock Desert, Nevada*, University of California, Department of Anthropology, Archeological Survey N. 73 (Berkeley).

6. Donald R. Tuohy, "Some Early Lithic Sites in Western Nevada," in *Eastern New Mexico University Contributions in Anthropology* (1968), 1:4.

CHAPTER II

The Desert's Nature

I T WAS LATE fall; soon winter storms would make travel on the big lake bed impossible. We had stopped on the playa to eat lunch, when a lone Brewer's blackbird coasted out of the sky to land less than twenty yards away. Cocking its head from side to side, its bright eyes watched us.

It was an unusual performance, and one of the party broke a piece of bread from his sandwich and tossed it in the direction of the bird. With almost no hesitation the feathered guest walked to it and began eating.

Several pieces of bread later, we continued on to another area of the desert. The car had hardly rolled to a stop when the blackbird landed beside it.

That evening we drove thirty miles to an over-night camp. On returning to the same general area the next morning, no one was really surprised to see a lone blackbird flying towards us as fast as its wings could propel it.

The Brewer's blackbird is noted for its fearless-ness. During the nesting season it will take on cats, dogs, hawks, or humans. Apparently it was hungry when it first came to us, but it was able to fly — and flying requires relatively enormous amounts of food energy. Its actions and why it was alone at that time of the year were never satisfactorily explained.

It was not a good example of the desert's living

things, but when someone claims that the lake bed is barren of life, we cannot help but think of that small black visitor.

The amount of available water acts as a basic control of the kinds and numbers of living things inhabiting a region, and this restriction is especially apparent in arid country. In the Great Basin the amount of precipitation varies with elevation and direction of slope. Pacific storm clouds, moving inland with prevailing westerly winds, cool and release moisture as they rise over mountain ranges, so that annual precipitation may be as high as twenty inches on the crest of a high mountain while only five inches on the adjoining valley floor.

The Quinn (originally Queen's) River enters the basin from the northeast and during spring runoff periods carries melted snow from distant northern mountains to the river's sink south of the Black Rock Range. There it spreads into a shallow but extensive sheet of water. By early summer, evaporation (which averages four feet annually) has sucked the temporary lake dry and reduced the river to occasional pools of muddy water.

Winter precipitation over the Black Rock region provides water for mountain springs, some of which feed streams flowing down canyons to the playa's edge. Thermal springs, with temperatures ranging from warm to boiling, have been well-known landmarks since the white man first came to the desert.

Plant life occurring on certain areas of the playa is generally limited to salt-tolerant species such as

KING LEAR PEAK OF THE JACKSON RANGE RISES TO MORE THAN 8,900 FEET
ABOVE SEA LEVEL.

various saltbushes and salt grasses. Some parts of
the playa, especially the northeastern sections, provide homes for many kinds of animals. Rodents,
insects, and even amphibians live both above and
below the dry mud surface. The desert's normal
stillness becomes a bedlam of sound when
thousands of cicada nymphs periodically emerge
from their underground way of life, and it is not
unusual to see a puddle of rainwater filled with the
tadpoles of a burrowing toad which is able to race
through its life history of egg to adult before the
pool of water dries.

The mountain ranges of the Black Rock region,

with peaks rising from 7,000 to 9,000 feet above sea level, form biologic islands. Moving up from the playa into the surrounding mountains, the vegetation changes into typical Great Basin shrubs such as sagebrush, shad-scale, greasewood, and rabbit brush.

At higher elevations sagebrush continues to be a dominant shrub, but the larger amounts of annual precipitation allow areas of aspen, mountain mahogany, and juniper trees on some mountains, as well as bitterbrush and various species of herbs and grasses which provide forage for wildlife and livestock.

Most of the animals found in other areas of the Great Basin Desert are either permanent or temporary residents of the Black Rock region. Big game mammals are mule deer and pronghorn antelope. Bighorn sheep, which once occupied many of Nevada's mountain ranges but have disappeared from most native areas, will be introduced into the Jackson Range (bordering the east side of the playa) and the Granite Range (which towers over Gerlach) if current plans materialize.

Carnivores, such as the coyote and bobcat, exist throughout most of the region, and the cougar (mountain lion) uses the Jackson and Pine Forest ranges as hunting areas. The small, largely nocturnal, kit fox had been seen out on the playa.

Canyons and springs of the region provide suitable habitat for game birds such as the native sage grouse and exotic chukar partridge.

Two kinds of fish are of special interest: a dace (kind of minnow) which is endemic to its stream in

Soldier Meadows and a pure strain of cutthroat trout for which Summit Lake is noted (see map). The high mountain lake lies within an Indian reservation, and federal fisheries personnel trap spawning trout and take the eggs to various hatcheries. The lake is closed to sport fishing.

Because the inner temperature of a reptile's body changes somewhat in relation to the outside temperature, the presence of a Great Basin rattlesnake on the playa where shade is not available would be very rare. In the surrounding mountains the rattler and several species of nonpoisonous snakes and lizards exist in about the same numbers as in other similar western areas.

The Black Rock region is not as barren as it might appear to a casual observer hurrying through it.

CHAPTER III

Its First Non-Indians

THEY WERE IN serious danger. It was midwinter; many of the horses and mules were
lame, their hoofs worn and cut by rocks, and they
were traveling through an unexplored region of
the Great Basin.

The party of twenty-five men had left The
Dalles on the Columbia River on November 25,
1843, to head southward. First paralleling the
eastern base of the Cascade Range, they had
turned east near Klamath Marsh and then south
again through an unknown region. During recent
days the country had been mountainous and
rough, at times deep in snow with bitter cold
nights. Two days ago they had seen "tracks where
a considerable party of Indians had passed on
horseback. . . ."[1]

Yesterday they had entered a narrow valley
(High Rock Canyon), and following a stream
which they believed would find its outlet in
"Mary's Lake"[2] they had come to an area where,
"On both sides, the mountain showed often
stupendous and curious-looking rocks, which at
several places so narrowed the valley that scarcely
a pass was left for the camp. It was a singular place
to travel through — shut up in the earth, a sort of
chasm, the little strip of grass under our feet, the

"ON BOTH SIDES, THE MOUNTAIN SHOWED OFTEN STUPEN-
DOUS AND CURIOUS-LOOKING ROCKS, WHICH AT SEVERAL
PLACES SO NARROWED THE VALLEY THAT SCARCELY A PASS
WAS LEFT FOR THE CAMP."
High Rock Canyon.

rough walls of bare rock on either hand, and the
narrow strip of sky above."

Now, on the last day of the year, they came to
the edge of the desert — the first non-Indians to
travel there.* John C. Fremont's journal noted,
"our new year's eve was rather a gloomy one. The
result of our journey began to be very uncertain;"

---

*Author's note: I discussed this with Gloria Griffen Cline, an authority on
Peter Skene Ogden, and she agreed that Ogden, in 1828, and John Work,
in 1831, may have passed close enough to the northeastern end of the Black
Rock Desert to have seen it, although their journals do not clearly show that
they entered the valley.

Belief in the existence of the legendary Buenaventura River, which was said to flow the Rocky Mountains to the Bay of San Francisco, had brought Fremont to this cold and lonely country. An earlier entry in his diary read, "In our journey across the desert, Mary's lake, and the famous Buenaventura river, were two points on which I relied to recruit the animals, and repose the party. Forming, agreeably to the best maps in my possession, a connected water line from the Rocky mountains to the Pacific Ocean, I felt no other anxiety than to pass safely across the intervening desert to the banks of the Buenaventura."

It would seem probable that Fremont's confidence in his maps might have begun to weaken, but on New Year's Day he again led his party southward down the leg of the Black Rock Desert which stretches between the Black Rock Range on the east and the Calico Mountains on the west. They followed the general course of a stream now known as Mud Meadows Creek, and today's description of most of the terrain would differ little from Fremont's account. "We continued down the valley, between a dry-looking black ridge on the left and a more snowy and high one on the right. Our road was bad along the bottom, being broken by gullies and impeded by sage, and sandy on the hills, where there is not a blade of grass, nor does any appear on the mountains. The soil in many places consists of a fine powdery sand, covered with a saline efflorescence; and the general character of the country is desert. During the day

Courtesy, Dr. Walter Orr Roberts

"DURING THE DAY WE DIRECTED OUR COURSE TOWARDS A BLACK CAPE, AT
THE FOOT OF WHICH A COLUMN OF SMOKE INDICATED HOT SPRINGS."

we directed our course towards a black cape,* at
the foot of which a column of smoke indicated hot
springs.

"January 2. — We were on the road early, the
face of the country hidden by falling snow. We
travelled along the bed of the stream, in some
places dry, in others covered with ice; the travelling being very bad, through deep fine sand, rendered tenacious by a mixture of clay. The weather
cleared up a little at noon, and we reached the hot
springs of which we had seen the vapor the day

---

*Author's note: The "black cape" must have been the Black Rock hill; there
is a hot spring at its base. Unless bad weather blocked it out, he should also
have seen steam from Double Hot Springs, approximately five miles north
of the Black Rock.

before. There was a large field of the usual salt grass here, peculiar to such places. The country otherwise is a perfect barren, without a blade of grass, the only plants being some dwarf Fremontias. We passed the rocky cape, a jagged broken point, bare and torn. The rocks are volcanic,[3] and the hills have a burnt appearance — cinders and coal occasionally appearing as at a blacksmith's forge. We crossed the large dry bed of a muddy lake in a southeasterly direction, and encamped at night without water and without grass, among sage bushes covered with snow."

The "bed of a muddy lake" was the sink of the Quinn River,[4] and travelling in a "southeasterly direction" to where there was sagebrush, would place their camp above the edge of the playa, probably somewhere near the course of today's Western Pacific Railroad tracks and west of the old station of Sulphur.

Most of the members of the party must have felt strong concern the next morning when they awakened to find the strange land covered with a "fog so dense that we could not see a hundred yards . . . the men that were sent out after the horses were bewildered and lost; . . . Our situation had now become a serious one. We had reached and run over the position where, according to the best maps in my possession, we should have found Mary's Lake or river. We were evidently on the verge of the desert which had been reported to us; and the appearance of the country was so forbidding, that I was afraid to enter it, and determined to bear away to the southward, keeping close along the mountains, in the full expectation of reaching the Buenaventura river."

Several mules and a horse had been lost the previous day and to lighten the loads of the remaining animals all members of the party traveled on foot, making their way "seven or eight miles along the ridge bordering the valley, and encamped where there were a few bunches of grass . . ."

Fremont's diary entry for January 4 indicates the growing effect of the fog on the morale of the party. "The fog today was still more dense, and the people again were bewildered. We travelled a few miles around the western point of the ridge, and encamped where there were a few tufts of grass, but no water. Our animals now were in a very alarming state, and there was increased anxiety in the camp."

Fortunately, while scouting the next day, a man named Taplin ascended a nearby mountain and, surprisingly, emerged into bright sunlight. On the following morning when Fremont climbed above the mist, the fog had thinned enough for him to see a high column of steam about sixteen miles distant to the southwest and, hoping for food for the animals, he determined to go there. Crossing the playa "over ground of yielding mud and sand" they came to "the most extraordinary locality of hot springs we had met during the journey."[5] There was an "abundance of grass, which, though only tolerably good, made this place, with reference to the past, a refreshing and agreeable spot."

That evening, doubtlessly prompted by the

happenings of the past few days, Fremont wrote, "Our situation now required caution. Including those which gave out from the injured condition of their feet, and those stolen by Indians, we had lost, since leaving the Dalles of the Columbia, fifteen animals; and of these, nine have been left in the last few days. I therefore determined, until we should reach a country of water and vegetation, to feel our way ahead, by having the line of route explored some fifteen or twenty miles in advance, and only to leave a present encampment when the succeeding one is known."

Following this plan, Fremont, accompanied by Kit Carson and a man named Godey, explored to the south until they found a satisfactory camping place with water and cottonwood trees alongside "a broad and plainly marked trail, on which there were tracks of horses, and we appeared to have regained one of the thoroughfares which pass by the watering places of the country."

The party remained at the Great Boiling Springs camp for another day to rest the livestock. "Mr. Preuss[6] had ascended one of the mountains, and occupied the day in sketching the country; and Mr. Fitzpatrick had found, a few miles distant, a hollow of excellent grass and pure water,[7] to which the animals were driven. . . . Indians appear to be every where prowling about like wild animals, and there is a fresh trail across the snow in the valley near."

On January 9 the camp was moved to the spring with the cottonwood trees.[8] While the party was enroute, Fremont and Carson reconnoitered the country ahead and found another good campsite for the following day.

"January 10. — We continued our reconnoisance ahead, pursuing a south direction in the basin along the ridge; the camp following slowly after. On a large trail there is never any doubt of finding suitable places for encampments. We reached the end of the basin, where we found, in a hollow of the mountain which enclosed it, an abundance of good bunch grass. Leaving a signal for the party to encamp, we continued our way up the hollow, intending to see what lay beyond the mountain. The hollow was several miles long, forming a good pass, the snow deepening to about a foot as we neared the summit. Beyond, a defile between the mountains descended rapidly about two thousand feet; and, filling up all the lower space, was a sheet of green water, some twenty miles broad. It broke upon our eyes like the ocean. The neighboring peaks rose high above us, and we ascended one of them to obtain a better view. The waves were curling in the breeze, and their dark-green color showed it to be a body of deep water. For a long time we sat enjoying the view, for we had become fatigued with mountains, and the free expanse of moving waves was very grateful."

They had reached Pyramid Lake, with the food and safety it offered. The difficulties of crossing the Sierra Nevada were still ahead, but at least the desert was behind them. The big playa had been kind to its first non-Indians.

NOTES TO CHAPTER III

1. There has been a general belief that the Indians of the Nevada section of the Great Basin did not use horses until they obtained them from the emigrants. However, Peter Skene Ogden reported that when his party was encamped near Humboldt Lake in May of 1829 one of his men was attacked by twenty Indians on horseback. See Gloria Griffen Cline, *Exploring the Great Basin*, University of Oklahoma Press, 1963; or "The Peter Skene Ogden Journals: Snake Country Expedition, 1827–28 and 1828–29," ed. T. C. Elliott, *Oregon Historical Quarterly*, vol. 2 (1910).

The relationship between the Northern Paiute and the Bannock Indians, discussed in Chapter 5, offers a possible explanation of Paiute horse-users.

2. The Humboldt River was first named Mary's River by Peter Skene Ogden. It is considered probable, but not certain, that John C. Fremont was referring to Humboldt Lake, in which the Humboldt River terminates.

3. Dr. Vincent P. Gianella, retired University of Nevada professor of geology, noted that the Black Rock is "volcanic dust rained down into the Permian sea millions of years ago. It contains Permian marine fossils. I collected them in 1959."

4. A heavy winter over the watershed of the Quinn River still results in a sheet of water which covers a large area of the sink. In the early days it was called Mud Lake.

5. Named Great Boiling Springs, they are located near the town of Gerlach, Nevada.

6. Mr. Charles Preuss was Fremont's cartographer. His published diary *Exploring With Fremont* does not have an entry for this day.

7. This could have been Granite Creek, approximately four miles northeast of the hot springs. It became the site of the Granite Creek station, made tragically famous by an Indian attack in 1865.

8. Rodeo Creek

CHAPTER IV

The Death Route

THEY SAT and stood around the fire, and by its light the thoughtful faces of the older men told of the importance of the decision which must now be made.*

During the past week rumors had come back along the line of wagons about a new trail which offered not only a shorter distance to the valleys of California but would bypass the dreaded Forty-Mile Desert. They had come to it this afternoon, the deeper ruts of the main road continuing along the river, the newer route branching to the right.

The older men were undecided and cautious. They had examined the tracks, and now they pointed out that for every wagon which had taken the new trail, hundreds had followed the old. Would it not be wiser, safer, they reasoned, to stay on the established route?

But the young men, welcoming a gamble which might save weeks, argued convincingly — basing

Author's note: This chapter, concerned with the 1849 Lassen emigrant route (later called Lassen's Horn Route, The Greenhorn Cutoff, and The Death Route) is not designed to provide new information for professional historians or experienced trail buffs. The summarized material, selected from accepted reliable sources, is primarily limited to the Black Rock Desert section of the long and hazardous journey. For readers who wish a concise account of the entire Lassen trail, George R. Stewart's excellent book, *The California Trail* (McGraw-Hill, 1962) is suggested.

Certainly the story of the desert could not be told without including the part it played in an important and exciting phase of Western history.

their logic on the perils of the desert now less then two days' travel ahead, and on the high mountain pass beyond it where the Donner tragedy had occurred three years before. Because of the lateness of the season, snow in the Sierra was a possibility, they said.

The fire had burned the last of its fuel before the decision was finally made. On the next morning, August 15, 1849, the wagons would turn to the right — to follow a trail which was destined to become known as "The Death Route."

The section of the new road, the part which stretched from the turnoff as far as Goose Lake on the California-Oregon border, had been first explored three years earlier by a party of fifteen Oregon men seeking a less hazardous route for emigrants to their country. Led by Jesse Applegate and traveling light on horseback, they left the Willamette Valley on the 20th of June, 1846. Although at times doubling back in search of better terrain, they reached the Goose Lake basin eighteen adventure-filled days later.

On July 9 the explorers crossed the Warner Mountains to enter beautiful Surprise Valley and, moving fast, were following Fremont's trail through High Rock Canyon the next day. On the 11th they came in sight of the big desert playa, and Lindsay Applegate (Jesse's brother) wrote, "The country eastward had a very forbidding appearance."[1] At Black Rock Spring the party rested for a day, and it is probable that they gave the dark hill its name. Lindsay wrote, "This place

IT IS PROBABLE THAT THE APPLEGATE BROTHERS GAVE THE
BLACK ROCK ITS NAME.

has ever since been known as Black Rock and is
one of the most noted landmarks. . . ."[2]

On July 14 the men split into two parties, one
riding southeasterly and the other more towards
the south, in an attempt to find the best route
from Black Rock to the Mary's (Humboldt) River.
Lindsay Applegate accompanied the group traveling southeast across the playa, and he reported
that after a fifteen-mile ride on an exceedingly hot
day both men and horses were suffering for need
of water when someone noticed rabbit trails, all
running in the same direction toward a ledge of
boulders. On reaching the ledge they found a
small hole in the top of a green mound "in which a

little puddle of water stood within a few inches of the surface." By digging a basin they were able to obtain enough water so that "by morning men and horses were considerably refreshed."

There seems little doubt that this small water seep, to which three years later emigrant diaries gave lasting fame, was named by the Applegate party. Lindsay wrote in his journal, "This is the place always since known as the Rabbit Hole Springs."

During the next several days, neither group was successful in finding a route with adequate water which would connect the California trail to Black Rock Spring. Continuing to search, the Oregonians traveled up the Humboldt River until on July 21 they came to a large meadow area, later named Lassen's Meadows. From there, looking to the west, they could see a mountain pass which they thought might offer a direct route to the Black Rock. On the following morning two of the party were sent to explore that possibility. When the men returned the next evening to report a spring[3] about fifteen miles from the meadows and approximately halfway to Rabbit Hole, a new route to Oregon was assured.

During the remainder of 1846 and during the next two years emigrants to Oregon successfully traveled the Applegate road. It was not until 1849, when thousands of humans used a section of it for a purpose for which it was not designed, that it became infamous.

PETER LASSEN, FAMOUS CALIFORNIA PIONEER.

It is not possible that one person alone was responsible for the misinformation which caused the 1849 disaster, but many historical accounts credit Peter Lassen with such an achievement.

Lassen, a blacksmith by trade, came to the United States from Denmark,[4] eventually reaching California, where in 1843 he received a grant of land in the northern section of the Sacramento Valley not far from present-day Vina on Deer Creek. Hoping to bring emigrants to his ranch and have them settle there, he traveled east in 1847 and in 1848 acted as a guide to a party of ten or twelve wagons bound for California. It is believed that he knew of the Applegate Trail but had not traveled it or explored the country beyond Goose Lake. However, when his party, traveling the main California Trail along the Humboldt River, came to the Applegate Trail intersection, Lassen took the north fork.

At Goose Lake he turned southward in the direction of his ranch, over terrain that was in places almost impassable. Details of the hardships the emigrants suffered are not fully known, but it is believed that many of them would not have survived had not a group of men traveling from Oregon to the gold fields in California overtaken the party somewhere beyond present-day Lake Almanor and helped them reach Lassen's ranch.

The trip from the turnoff at Lassen's Meadows required approximately two months, yet early in 1849 the route was promoted as a shorter and easier way to the Sacramento Valley. Even the *New York Herald* carried a report, allegedly formulated

LASSEN'S ROUTE.

by some members of the Lassen party, which
praised both the route and the man who had
guided them along it.

And so it was that in mid-August 1849 wagons
began turning off the main California trail to take
a route that would soon make the Black Rock
playa a notorious desert.

In April of 1849 men of all occupations, some
accompanied by their families, gathered along the
banks of the Missouri River at Independence, St.
Joseph, Council Bluffs, and Old Fort Kearny, waiting for prairie grass to mature enough to provide
food for draft animals. The wagons started west
during the last few days of April, and by mid-June
an estimated 22,000 people[5] were moving along
the trail, bound for California and the goldfields.

By August 11 approximately half the travelers
had passed the Applegate-Lassen turnoff to continue down the Humboldt River and follow either
the Truckee or Carson river routes to the Sacramento Valley. The remainder had not yet
reached Lassen's Meadows when a well-known
guide led his wagons off the main trail onto the
year-old tracks made by Lassen's party and emigrants bound for Oregon. Soon hundreds of other
wagons were turning to the right, so that suddenly
a large part of the year's migration had been rerouted to a trail which, instead of providing a
shortcut to the goldfields, was almost 200 miles
farther than the established roads.

Many of the travelers kept diaries, most of
which provide little detail. There are two journals

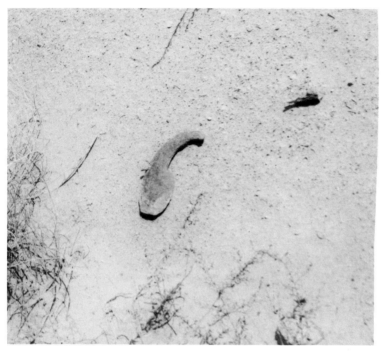

A WELL PRESERVED OX SHOE ON THE HUMBOLDT EMIGRANT
TRAIL.

which are especially admired by many amateur
and professional historians. Alonzo Delano (a dry
goods merchant from Illinois who would become
California's first well-known writer) reached
Lassen's Meadows on August 15, 1849, and his account of the journey is an easily read, interesting
narrative.[6] J. Goldsborough Bruff, a former West
Pointer and civilian cartographer, arrived at the
meadow turnoff on September 19, more than a
month after Delano. His excellent journal[7] provides the detailed observations which currently

allow history buffs to follow the old trail accurately and understand the hardships its 1849 travelers suffered.

Delano's party, on reaching Lassen's Meadows, listened to conflicting reports about the new trail. "It was decided, finally, that we would go the northern route, although some of our company had misgivings. The younger portion, being fond of adventure, were loud in favor of the road."

Deciding to travel at night when temperatures would be cooler for the oxen, the company started for Rabbit Hole Springs on the evening of August 15. Delano and a companion, Mr. Fredenburg, walked ahead of the wagons in a "northwest direction, across the plain towards a gorge, through which the road ran. . . ." By 11:00 P.M. they had covered twelve miles and reached the first springs (Antelope Springs), where they spread their blankets and slept.

Daylight showed us nothing but rugged barren mountains; and instead of the grass we had been assured of, there was not a blade to be seen. All that there had been grew on a little moist place, irrigated by three small springs, and this trifle had been consumed by earlier trains. . . . Our wagons had passed during the night. . . . It was now twenty miles or more to Rabbit Springs, the next water."

Feeling anxious about the oxen's need of water, Delano hurried along the trail, eventually catching up with and passing his train. Along the way he admired "the most beautiful hills of colored earth I ever saw, with the shades of pink, white, yellow,

SEATED ON THE EDGE OF RABBIT HOLE SPRING, CRAIG MAKES HIS SKETCH
FOR THE PAINTING ON PAGE 70.

and green brightly blended. Volcanic mountains were around us, and under ordinary circumstances we could have enjoyed the strange and peculiar scenery."

Disappointment and concern awaited at Rabbit Hole Springs. ". . . we found the promised springs to be only three or four wells sunk in the ground, into which the water percolated in a volume about the size of a straw, and each hole occupied by a

man dipping it up with a pint cup, as it slowly filled a little cavity in the ground."

With no possibility of obtaining enough water
for the oxen, Delano's company now faced a serious decision. "Beyond us, far as we could see, was
a barren waste, without a blade of grass or a drop
of water for thirty miles at least. Instead of avoiding the desert, instead of the promised water,
grass, and a better road, we were in fact upon a
more dreary and wider waste. . . . We had been
inveigled there by false reports and misrepresenta-
tion, without preparing for such a contingency, as
we might have done, in some measure, by cutting
grass on the river. Our train came up, followed by
others. What was to be done? It was thirty-five
miles to the river and about the same distance to
the spring ahead. Should we go back? Our cattle
had already gone without food or water for nearly
thirty hours. Could they stand it to go back? Could
they possibly go forward?

"While we were deliberating, four wagons came
in from the west on their return. They had driven
ten miles on the plain, and seeing no probability of
reaching water, they commenced a retrograde
movement for the river. A few of our older men
hesitated, and were of the opinion that prudence
dictated that we should return to the river, where
we were sure of the means of going forward,
rather than launch into the uncertainties before
us. But the majority, without knowing anything of
the geography of the country, decided that they
might as well go forward as back — trusting to
luck more than to judgement — a measure which

FROM A RISE IN FRONT OF RABBIT HOLE, THEY COULD SEE THE BLACK ROCK.

reduced us to weeks of continued toil and increased hardships. We came to the determination that we would wait until near sunset, as the cattle could travel better without water in the night than by daylight."

The company left Rabbit Hole Springs about six o'clock that evening, "with anxious hearts and sad forebodings, on our perilous journey."

About midnight Delano turned aside from the road to sleep "till the morning sun was shining on my eyelids."

"As I walked on slowly and with effort, I encountered a great many animals, perishing for want of food and water, on the desert plain. Some would be gasping for breath, others unable to stand, would issue low moans as I came up, in a most distressing manner, showing intense agony; . . . while here or there a poor ox or horse, just able to drag himself along, would stagger towards me with a low sound as if begging for a drop of water. My sympathies were excited at their sufferings, yet, instead of affording them aid, I was a subject for relief myself.

"High above the plain, in the direction of our road, a black, bare mountain reared its head, at the distance of fifteen miles; and ten miles this side the plain was flat, composed of baked earth, without a sign of vegetation, and in many places covered with incrustations of salt. Pits had been sunk in moist places, but the water was salt as brine, and utterly useless. Before leaving Rabbit Springs I had secured about a quart of water, in an india-rubber flask, which I had husbanded with great care. When few miles from Black Rock Spring, I came to a wagon, standing in the road, in which was seated a young woman, with a child. The little boy was crying for water, and the poor mother, with the tears running down her cheeks, was trying to pacify the little sufferer.

" 'Where is your husband?' I inquired, on going up.

" 'He has gone on with the cattle,' she replied, 'and to try to get us some water, but I think we shall die before be comes back. It seems as if I could not endure it much longer.'

" 'Keep up a stout heart,' I returned, 'a few more miles will bring us in, and we shall be safe. I have a little water left: I am strong and can walk in — you are welcome to it.'

" 'God bless you — God bless you,' said she, grasping the flask eagerly, 'Here, my child — here is water!" and before she had tasted a drop her-

AT FIRST IT IS HARD TO BELIEVE THAT THOUSANDS OF TRAVELERS PASSED OVER THIS ROAD MORE THAN 125 YEARS AGO.

self, she gave her child nearly all, which was but little more than a teacup. Even in distress and misery, a mother's love is for her children, rather than for herself."

Delano's train reached the hot spring near the Black Rock about nine o'clock in the morning. The spring irrigated approximately twenty acres of land, but there again the grass had already been nearly consumed. Water within the spring was too hot to touch, but where it overflowed into a natural basin and cooled, it afforded Delano and others an opportunity to bathe, "which we found exceedingly refreshing."

Learning that there was another "oasis" several miles farther north, the company decided to go on that evening. "Just before starting, I climbed to the top of Black Rock hill. As I ascended towards the summit, the air grew cold, and on the top I was met by a rain and hail storm, which chilled me through, though only a few drops fell at the base. I was glad to hurry down into a warmer climate, and follow in the wake of our train."

Based on Delano's description, the party camped overnight at what is now called Double Hot Springs. ". . . about fifty teams lying over to recruit their cattle, after having lost a good many in the transit to Black Rock Spring."

During the day of August 18, a supply of grass was cut to carry along in case of emergency, and all of the kegs were filled with water. "Our cattle being recruited, we left about sunset, and were soon plowing our way ankle-deep in the yielding sand. Quite a number of men walked ahead. . . .

The route Delano followed was on the eastern side of the desert floor and became the main trail. It should not be confused with the present dirt road along the foothills of the Black Rock Range which may have been started by Hardin City miners when the desert was set, and later used by ranchers. In September many emigrants cut across the desert for the fresh water of Donnelly Creek and then traveled up the west side until they intersected the east trail below Soldier Meadows.

THE OLD TRAIL STILL HEADS FOR THE BLACK ROCK.

When we arrived where we thought our morning walk would be easy, we lay down in the sand to rest, but the cold night air and the howling of the hungry wolves, who would have made us bosom friends if they could, prevented sleep."

The company reached "a kind of wet valley, containing several hundred acres of excellent grass and plenty of good water" the next day, August 19. This area is now known as Soldier Meadows.

"We were now across the desert proper, . . . Instead of avoiding the desert, as we fondly anticipated when we left the Humboldt; instead of getting rid of a forty-five mile sand-plain, we had actually crossed the desert where it was a hundred miles broad, and in comparison, we should have looked upon the other route as a play-spell."

Shortly after reaching the meadows, Delano's party learned that Indians had been troublesome, killing a horse and a mule and driving off several head of cattle the night before.

"We kept a strict guard during the night, and all the companies were on the alert; yet, notwithstanding all our caution, the Indians came down from the hills and drove off one cow and horse, and badly wounded two more horses, . . . One of the horses was shot in the side and died during the day; in the other, the stone pointed arrow had

THIS HOT SPRING NEAR THE BLACK ROCK WAS THE FIRST GOAL OF TRAVELERS LEAVING RABBIT HOLE SPRINGS.

HILLOCKS OF DRY MUD SEPARATE THE PLAYA FROM THE BLACK ROCK.

completely perforated the back bone — with such amazing force do they shoot these arrows."

As protection against possible Indian attacks it was decided that several trains should travel together, and on the morning of August 21 a group of about twenty-five wagons, including Delano's party, moved out of Soldier Meadows and, after being let down into a canyon by ropes, "came to the entrance of one of the most remarkable curiosities among the mountains. It was [High Rock Canyon] a cañon, or narrow, rocky pass through the mountains, just wide enough for a smooth, level road, with intervals of space occasionally, to afford grass and water. On each side were walls of perpendicular rock, four or five hundred feet high. . . . Without this singular avenue, a passage across the mountains in this vicinity would have been impossible, and it seemed as if

Providence, forseeing the wants of his creatures, had in mercy opened this strange path, by which they could extricate themselves from destruction and death."

Twenty-eight days of difficult travel remained ahead for Delano's company, but they had started early and the barren desert was behind them. On September 17 they reached Lassen's ranch. J. Goldsborough Bruff, with his company of sixty-six men and seventeen wagons, had not yet arrived at Lassen's Meadows.

Because Bruff attentively observed and carefully recorded so much along the trail, his journal has been of much value to historians and researchers. Also, his position toward the rear of the great migration allowed a description of the conditions late travelers faced. By September 19, the day Bruff's company arrived at the Lassen's Meadows turnoff, many changes had taken place along the route.

At the junction Bruff found the trails as "broad and as well beaten as any traveled thoroughfare can be."[8] A barrel, painted red and labeled "post office" and half filled with letters, stood in the forks of the road. On the left of the trail was the grave of a three-year-old girl.

The company had not traveled far along the dusty road before Bruff had tallied "twenty-two dead oxen, and two dead horses, and countless wheels, hubs, tires, and other fragments of wagons, ox-yokes, bows, chains, &c."

There was more available water for the late

HIGH ROCK CANYON.

IN HIGH ROCK CANYON, WAGON WHEELS WORE RUTS IN ROCK.

travelers than for earlier ones. At Antelope Springs small reservoirs had been built to allow animals to drink, and at Rabbit Hole Springs the wells had been deepened and widened.

Rabbit Hole Springs was an unpleasant place for the late arrivals. Bruff counted eighty-two dead oxen, two dead horses, and a mule within an area of one-tenth of a mile. The bloated bodies of dead oxen filled two of the wells; the headboard on a fresh grave told of a fifty-year-old man from Ohio who had died of camp fever.

It may have been here that many emigrants fully realized the dangers — the possible horrors

RABBIT HOLE SPRINGS WAS AN UNPLEASANT PLACE FOR THE LATER ARRIVALS. BRUFF COUNTED 82 DEAD OXEN, 2 DEAD HORSES AND A MULE WITHIN AN AREA OF $^1/_{10}$ OF A MILE.

Courtesy Inez Johnson

HIGH ROCK CANYON HAS CHANGED VERY LITTLE SINCE TRAVELERS LEFT
THEIR NAMES THERE.

— they faced. It was an environment which should
have brought realization — the suffocating stench
of decomposing animal bodies, the wreckage of
wagons, and from a nearby rise an opportunity to
see, far in the distance, the Black Rock hill and the
barren desert which must be crossed to reach it.
To many it was a moment of decision — whether
to turn back to the Humboldt River or continue
on into unknown country and hazards.

Bruff, an exceptionally competent captain of his
train, had been cautious enough to cut grass at
Lassen's Meadows and store it in his wagons. Few
of the other parties had taken this precaution,

and, with no forage left in the neighborhood, some were baking bread to feed their animals.

Before moving out on the morning of September 21, Bruff was involved in an incident which could have ended tragically had he been a man with less self-discipline. "A young man of the company, as reckless as unprincipled, backed by several scoundrels, attempted this morning to take my horse, prompt determination frustrated them. The recollection of their parents stayed my hand as I was on the eve of making a bloody example. Glad that I checked myself."

The general descriptions of the trail to the Black Rock are similar. Although the pull was largely downhill to the edge of the lake bed, even that section of the road was lined with the carcasses of oxen, the wreckage of abandoned wagons and carts (some of which had been burned), "and every kind of property."

On the edge of the playa many emigrants may have paused for a moment on an ancient beach terrace to stare out across a great flat of dried mud. They would have known that the dark mounds which dotted the lake bed were more bodies of dead and dying animals.

Less than a mile out on the playa, the travelers would have had to cross the stream bed of the Quinn River, and it is interesting to note that, of the diaries read, none mention the channel. In 1849 there were no ranches to divert, or reservoirs to store, the waters of the river. Yet today, with men upstream using most of the water, the channel is dangerous to cross in the fall of a normal

ON THE EDGE OF THE PLAYA, FROM AN ELEVATED ANCIENT
BEACH TERRACE, THEY COULD SEE THE BARREN FLAT THEY
MUST CROSS.

precipitation year. Cars have broken through the
crust of dry or moist mud and become so deeply
mired that even tow trucks had difficulty extricat-
ing them. At least in northern Nevada, 1849 must
have been an extremely dry year.

Those who had crossed the desert in August
suffered most from the heat, but even in mid-
September the afternoon sun forced many to walk
in the shadows of the wagons. As the emigrants
moved farther out onto the desert the amount of
abandoned material suggested that fear and hardship had, in many cases, resulted in panic.

Bruff recorded, "A very beautiful Mirage in the

south, southwest on this plain, at the base of some mountains. In which appeared a long lagoon of light blue water, bordered with tall trees, small islands and their reflection in its delightful looking bosom. . . . Oxen had stampeded for it, hoping to quench their burning thirst, and left their swelled-up carcasses over the plain in that direction, as far as we could discern them."

It was after sunset when Bruff's company reached the hot spring at the Black Rock. There he counted 150 dead oxen, 3 horses and 5 mules as well as the usual remains of wagons.

Late the next morning, September 22, after examining "the extraordinary Volcanic Cliffs, called the 'Black Rock' — the upper portion of which is a perfect rookery, filled with thousands of crows and ravens," Bruff continued onward. When passing Double Hot Springs his mules demonstrated why they are considered, by people who know them well, both intelligent and humorous animals. "We reached a pretty clear sparkling rill, about six feet broad, and a few inches deep: when to my astonishment the mules halted short at the edge, and refused, in spite of my whip and shouting, to put a foot in! — I guessed there might be a vapor from it, but on putting my hand in, found it quite hot — not sufficiently to scald, however. So we had much trouble here, pulling and urging the teams over; and when they did go, it was accomplished by each pair of mules, in succession, leaping over like deer, and thus jerking the wagons after them."

Bruff's journal strongly indicates that the trail

A MODERN WAGON TRAIN MAKES A LUNCH STOP WITH "FREMONT'S CASTLE" (HIGHEST WHITE FORMATION ON MOUNTAINSIDE) IN BACKGROUND.

turned across the playa to the lower reaches of a stream now called Donnelly Creek.[9] Here they found ". . . plenty of pretty good grass, — on the sides of a considerable brook of good clear water."

On the next day Bruff recorded and sketched a landmark which modern trail buffs often look for. "From our position at noon across the valley to the north by west was a very remarkable resemblance of a castle or fortress, of a white substance (probably clay), on the face of a brownish hill, resting on a shelf of rock, about ⅓ from the plain. This I sketch'd and named it Fremont's Castle."[10]

On the morning of September 24 Bruff moved

on, leaving the Black Rock Desert behind on September 25. The remainder of his recorded story contains many accounts of hardship and tragedy. Winter storms, loss of livestock to Indians, lack of food, and illness descended upon the thousands of struggling, exhausted humans who had turned onto the wrong trail — at the wrong time of year.

There is little doubt that 1849 would be remembered for one of this country's great tragedies if it had not been for the courageous and selfless efforts of rescue parties sent out from California by military governor General P. F. Smith and organized and led by Major D. H. Rucker and civilian J. H. Peoples.

Bruff's journey ended short of his goal when his

DURING A FIELD TRIP OF THE TRAILS WEST ORGANIZATION, DR. VINCENT GIANELLA *(left)* DISCUSSES A SECTION OF THE APPLEGATE-LASSEN TRAIL WITH JIM LINEBAUGH OF SURPRISE VALLEY.

company abandoned its wagons in the foothills of the Sacramento Valley, about twenty-six miles northeast of present Vina. The conscientious captain remained with the property during the winter, an ordeal which almost cost him his life.

A strong will allowed the survival of this unusual man — and the preservation of his remarkable journal.

In higher areas, many sections of the old road can still be seen and in some places followed in automobiles. But on the playa itself, winds and winter storms have erased the deep ruts once dug by hundreds of California- and Oregon-bound wagons. Only the diaries and a hill of black rock remain to tell the location of the desert trail.

NOTES FOR CHAPTER IV

1. Lindsay Applegate, "The Applegate Route in the Year 1846," *Oregon Historical Society Quarterly*, vol. 22 (1921).

2. In several places further along in his journal Lindsay uses the term "Black Hole."

3. Antelope Springs.

4. R. J. Swartzlow, *Lassen: His Life and Legacy*," published in cooperation with the National Park Service, Loomis Museum Association (Fairfield, Calif., 1964).

5. George R. Stewart, using data from various sources, calculated that approximately 22,500 people traveled the trail in 1849.

6. Alonzo Delano, *Across the Plains and Among the Diggins* (University Microfilms, a Xerox Company).

7. *Gold Rush: The Journals, Drawings, and Other Papers of J. Goldsborough Bruff*, ed. Georgia Willis Read and Ruth P. Gaines, 2 vols. (New York: Columbia University Press, 1944) by permission of the publisher.

8. Ibid.

9. Except for man's changes affecting the lower part of the stream, it is amazing how closely Bruff's description fits this area today.

10. Fremont's Castle can be seen on the south face of Paiute Peak in the Black Rock Range.

CHAPTER V

The Desert's Indian War

WHILE STUDYING the military reports, newspaper articles, and letters written between March 1865 and January 1866, a researcher may wonder whether they originally provided the plots for many twentieth century motion pictures. The leading characters are all there: the fierce Indian chief; the young, inexperienced, error-prone officer; the Indian scout who turned the military's tide of defeat; and even "Gunsmoke's" civilian medical doctor.

Conflict between the Northern Paiute Indian and the white man had begun approximately thirty-three years earlier at the sink of the Humboldt River when Joseph Walker's party of beaver trappers fired into a band of Indians, killing more than thirty of them. The order to fire was given not because the Indians were attacking or definitely threatening to do so; the decision was made merely on the basis that there was a large number of Indians who might surround the party unless the whites demonstrated their strength.

During his 1843-44 expedition, Fremont encountered no hostility from the Northern Paiutes, and five years later, except for loss of stock, the swarm of emigrants crossing the Black Rock desert experienced little harm from these native people.

A statement by Captain William Weatherlow,[1] a highly respected leader in Honey Lake Valley, contains information concerning Indian-white relationships from 1855 through 1858 in Honey Lake Valley, the nearest white settlement to the Black Rock-Smoke Creek Desert. Weatherlow pointed out that when he first settled in the valley the Paiutes occupied that area in common with the whites, and "were upon the most friendly terms with them, visiting the houses of the whites and trading furs and game for such articles of clothing, etc. as they desired. They were unlike other tribes I had met in as much as they were never known to beg for food or clothing nor did they at every opportunity pilfer or carry off articles from the settlement. They were under the command and control of Winnemucca [Numaga, often called Young Winnemucca], the present war Chief and faithfully obeyed his orders. There was a small band however which lived in or near Smoke Creek Canyon and were under the control of a Chief known as Smoke Creek Sam. These had in a measure drawn away from Winnemucca's band. . . . In 1855 the settlers of the valley made a treaty with Chief Winnemucca, the terms of which were that if any Indian committed any depredation or stole anything from the whites, the settlers should go to the chief and make complaint to him and not take their [sic] revenge indiscriminately upon the Indians, and the whites on their part agreed that if a white man should steal horses or cattle from the Indians or molest their squaws that the chief should come and make his complaint and the settler would redress his wrongs and punish the offender. . . . The treaty was faithfully observed on both sides, and never in a single instance was there a misunderstanding between the whites and the Indians.

"From the first settlement of the valley the Pitt River Indians which inhabit the Country north of Honey Lake had made frequent incursions upon the settlements — driven off stock and committed other outrages. In the year 1857, I raised a company of sixty men and went out against the Pitt River tribe on several occasions when they made descent upon the valley — Winnemucca volunteered to go with his warriors and aid us in fighting the Pitt River Indians — his offer was accepted and he and his warriors placed themselves under my command and rendered most efficient service. . . . On one occasion we succeeded in surprising some three hundred of the Pitt River Indians as they were in the act of massacring a small train of Mormon Emigrants; we made a descent upon the Indians killed some 25 of them and put the rest to flight, recovered the stock they had stolen and escorted the emigrant families to the settlement."

It was not until the spring of 1859 that an event seriously tested the relations between Honey Lake Valley settlers and the Northern Paiute Indians — and created a mystery which after 118 years still remains unsolved and controversial.*

*Author's note: This story of Peter Lassen's death combines information from three principal sources: On April 30, 1859, four days after the murder, Mr. F. N. (or Z. N.) Spaulding of Honey Lake Valley wrote a report which was published in the Downieville, California, Mountain Messenger

In July of 1858 a party of men led by James Allen Hardin unsuccessfully searched the Black Rock Range for a silver deposit which Hardin believed he had discovered in 1849 when he was a member of a wagon train following the Applegate-Lassen Trail through the desert.[2]

During the ensuing winter Peter Lassen, who had moved to Honey Lake Valley four years earlier, joined with Captain Weatherlow and five other men to plan another prospecting expedition to the Black Rock mountains. By midspring preparations were completed, and on April 17 Captain Weatherlow with three men started the long trip. Lassen with two men, Lemericus Wyatt and Edward Clapper, followed two days later. Plans called for the two groups to rendezvous at a place on the west side of the Black Rock Range.

Lassen's party was adequately outfitted. Two pack mules were loaded with food supplies, prospecting tools, blankets, and even a small keg of whiskey. The three men had good mounts. Lassen was noted for his fine horses and rode one named Wild Tom, "a high strung and spirited animal, but gentle and noted for his intelligence."[3] The men carried rifles.

They followed the Honey Lake-Humboldt River

---

newspaper and reprinted in Hutchings' *California Magazine* of June 1859. Thirty-four years later, December 3, 1893, the *San Francisco Chronicle* devoted two full columns of its front page to a story carrying the headline, "Peter Lassen's Death — An Authentic Story Of His Murder," which claimed to be the account Lemericus Wyatt had told his employer, Ephraim V. Spencer, many times. The third source is an unpublished paper written by F. F. Kingsbury, the son of a prominent Honey Lake Valley pioneer, W. C. Kingsbury, who was Peter Lassen's ranching partner.

Trail, eventually dropping down Smoke Creek Canyon to the edge of the desert. For the next few days they rode northeastward, using the playa where it was dry and moving to higher ground to bypass long stretches of lake bed still muddy from the past winter's rain and snow. Before reaching the Black Rock hill they turned north to follow or parallel the old emigrant trail which Lassen had helped to make notorious eleven years before. Late in the afternoon of the twenty-fourth they came to the base of a mountain (now named Paiute Peak) where they expected to meet the Weatherlow party. A preliminary search was unsuccessful, and with evening approaching Lassen entered a canyon where there was a small stream of water and made camp under rock bluffs.

The following morning Clapper rode "eight" miles to Mud Lake looking for Weatherlow's camp but found no trace. Later in the day the footprints of two white men and the tracks of shod horses were found in the vicinity of the Lassen camp, indicating that Weatherlow was either farther up the mountain or had crossed over the ridge to the other side of the range. The three men decided to spend another night at their present camp and continue the search the next morning.

While cooking supper they saw an Indian on horseback circling the camp. After some hesitancy he dismounted and came close enough to make it known that he needed powder, caps, and shot for the muzzle-loading rifle which he carried. Wyatt and Clapper strongly objected to furnishing ammunition, but Lassen, who said the Indian spoke

Paiute, gave him a supply of the items requested, and the Indian rode off.

At dawn the next morning Wyatt was awakened by the report of a rifle. Jumping to his feet, he called to his companions. When Clapper did not respond, Wyatt turned him onto his back and saw that he had been shot through the head.

Wyatt started to run for the horses, calling for Lassen to follow. But Lassen delayed, attempting to locate the place from which the rifle shot had originated. There was a second shot and Lassen fell.

Wyatt turned back to Lassen and partly raised him from the ground. Then, realizing that nothing could be done for him, he again ran for the horses, only to find they had pulled their picket ropes and stampeded. As he continued running toward the desert where a cloud of dust marked the path of the runaway horses, a bullet passed through a leg of his trousers.

Wyatt, sixty years old and weighing over two hundred pounds, was slow on his feet. Without a horse he knew he could not escape.

According to the San Francisco *Chronicle* story, "As he peered hopelessly after the retreating cloud he saw something which made his heart leap into his mouth. Out of the dust the form of his own fine, black pacing horse[4] suddenly appeared. The animal had faced about, apparently struck by some sudden impulse. For a second or two it seemed to take its bearings, and then on a mad gallop retraced its steps until it reached the advancing Wyatt and invited the old man as plainly as signs could indicate to mount."

Wyatt rode the more than one hundred and twenty miles to Honey Lake Valley without a saddle and without food or rest.

Captain Weatherlow wrote, "The killing of Lassen and his companion caused great excitement in the settlement and much feeling against the Indians. Several of the settlers attributed the murder to the Pah-utes [Paiutes], but from my own knowledge of the friendly relations between Chief Winnemucca and Peter Lassen and the high estimation in which Lassen was held by the Indians, and from the fact that there was no apparent change in the conduct of the Pah-utes who contrived to visit our houses and exchange civilities and friendships, I did not believe the Pah-utes had committed the murder nor that they were at all cognizant of the fact. I attributed it all to the Pitt River Tribe. . . ."

The Indian agent, Major F. Dodge, after talking to Indians and Chief Winnemucca, questioned whether any Indians had been involved. He pointed out that two sacks of flour, dried beef, blankets, and part of a keg of whiskey had not been taken from the deserted camp. A newspaper reported that Dodge believed Lassen was killed by white men. The story spread rapidly.

Fairfield wrote, "At first a good many believed it, but in a short time very few put any faith in the story. The writer, however, has met one or two men who believe it to this day, and they think they have good reasons for doing so."

Fariss and Smith in the 1882 *History of Plumas,*

FOR SEVERAL YEARS LIBRARIAN KENNETH CARPENTER, A FRE-
QUENT VISITOR TO THE BLACK ROCK DESERT, HAS FRUITLESSLY
SEARCHED FOR CLAPPER'S GRAVE.

Lassen, and Sierra Counties, California, wrote, "The
Indians were charged with his murder, but it is a
question whether the perpetrators of the deed
were not of the Caucasian race."

Fred F. Kingsbury wrote, "In the history of Lassen County . . . it states that Indians killed Peter
Lassen under a bluff in the Black Rock district of
Nevada. . . . But my father, W. C. Kingsbury, who
was a partner of Peter Lassen at the time of his
death, always said Peter was killed by a white man
and not an Indian, and several years later I over-
heard a drunken man make a remark that sub-
stantiated my father's opinion, before his friend
stopped him. . . .

"Also they used an Indian for a decoy — namely when the party camped at night an Indian dropped in on them to ascertain if Peter Lassen was there. . . .

"In 1859 very few Indians had rifles; they did not molest anything in camps or take any scalps. Chief Winnemucca and his braves were Masonic brothers and very friendly to Peter Lassen. . . ."[5]

Why, when the murders occurred in Indian country, did many settlers believe a white man or men killed Lassen and Clapper? Did the party of Honey Lake Valley men who traveled to the Black Rock Desert to bury the two bodies find evidence (perhaps tracks of a shod horse) which convinced at least some of them that Indians were not involved? Apparently they did some investigating; Fairfield states, "Everything went to show the truth of Wyatt's statement."[6]

After 118 years it is unlikely that the mystery will ever be solved. But there is another consideration.

Peter Lassen, for whom a mountain, a California county, and a national forest are named, was a famous western pioneer. Most historical records state that he was killed by Indians, a conclusion which may be correct or false. If false, it is an injustice which inaccurate history will preserve for generation after generation. Shouldn't the records have read "killed by person or persons unknown?"

During the first month of 1860 the friendly peace which had existed between the Northern Paiutes and the people of Honey Lake Valley suddenly ended when Indians of the Smoke Creek band, under the leadership of Smoke Creek Sam, killed a settler, Dexter E. Deming. Captain Weatherlow traveled to Pyramid Lake to request Chief Winnemucca to honor the long-standing treaty under which the murders of Deming could be punished. Winnemucca refused to cooperate.

During the following few months thousands of whites rushed to the new, rich silver mines at Virginia City, and among them were men who mistreated the Indians with whom they came in contact. It was probably the kidnapping of two Paiute women which started the final chain of events leading to the May 12 battle of Pyramid Lake in which more white men died than in any prior white-Indian engagement in the Far West.[7]

On June 2 the second battle of Pyramid Lake resulted in the withdrawal of the Indian forces to the north, possibly to the Black Rock Desert. Later in the year Colonel Frederick W. Lander met with Young Winnemucca (Numaga) and established a basis for peace between the whites and the main body of northwestern Nevada Paiutes.

To provide a military headquarters in the Nevada Territory, construction of Fort Churchill on the Carson River was begun in mid-1860. Approximately 200 men manned the fort during its first months of operation, but in 1861 the regular army units were moved east to participate in the Civil War, leaving the Nevada Territory almost unprotected from both Indians and Confederate supporters. Fortunately 1861 was a year of relative peace between Indians and non-Indians.

In neighboring California, companies of volunteers were quickly recruited to replace regular army units; and (primarily to preserve the Nevada Territory's loyalty to the Union) the Department of the Pacific, with headquarters at the Presidio of San Francisco, sent California Volunteers to Fort Churchill. In November of 1861, Major Charles McDermit of the Second California Volunteer Cavalry was placed in command of the fort.

The relative peace between Indians and whites enjoyed during 1861 was temporarily suspended during the next year, especially in the neighborhood of the road from Honey Lake to the Humboldt River which passed through the Black Rock Desert basin. This heavily traveled overland route had been discovered ten years earlier when a prospector named William Nobles traveled from Honey Lake eastward through Smoke Creek Canyon to intersect the Applegate Trail near the Black Rock. Believing he had found a direct and easier route to the upper Sacramento Valley, he returned to California where he obtained support from Shasta City businessmen.

First attempts to persuade people using the old Humboldt Trail to try the new route failed because the first part of it, as far as the Black Rock, followed the infamous Lassen route. Eventually an emigrant party was successfully guided across it, and soon its advantages over other roads to northern California were realized.

The original Nobles road branched from the Applegate Trail at the hot springs at Black Rock to head southwest to Granite Creek (near today's town of Gerlach). Later, a shortcut resulted when the turnoff was moved back to Rabbit Hole Springs and the road rerouted to parallel the southeast edge of the desert in a more direct heading for Granite Springs. During the fall of 1859 and the spring 1860 the federal government sent Col. Frederick W. Lander with a company of men to improve the road between Honey Lake and the Humboldt River.

During 1862 the Nobles road had one distinct disadvantage — it passed through country used as a refuge by one or more bands of hostile Indians.[8] Stations offering food and liquor to travelers had been set up along the road and because of their

Courtesy Nevada Historical Society, Alice Addenbrooke Collection
COLONEL CHARLES McDERMIT AND HIS FAMILY.

isolation were especially open to attack. In March
a hired man temporarily living alone at the Deep
Hole station (see map) was killed; his body was
found in a spring pond. Early in April the Mud
Flat station was burned.

Other attacks on travelers which resulted in the
deaths of both whites and Indians and the theft of
cattle and horses in Honey Lake Valley brought
complaints to Nevada Territory Governor Nye
which resulted in a promise by Brigadier General
Wright, commanding the U.S. Army Department
of the Pacific, that a permament army cavalry post
would be placed in the threatened area. By the
spring of 1863 the post had been established at
Smoke Creek and manned by California Volunteer troops from Fort Crook.

In April of 1863 General Wright requested the
acting governor, Orion Clemens, to recruit and
organize two Nevada volunteer companies of
cavalry and two of infantry. Nevadans responded to
the need, and by the spring of 1864, four companies of cavalry and four of infantry, totaling approximately 500 men had been mustered in at
Fort Churchill. The California troops at the
Smoke Creek post were relieved of their assign-
ment when twenty-five men and one officer of
Company D, First Cavalry, Nevada Volunteers arrived there in October of 1863. It was a remote
and lonely place, and the old records tell of men
deserting — only to be tracked down across the
desert and, after trading shots with their white
pursuers, surrendering.

In the microfilm files of letters to the Commis-

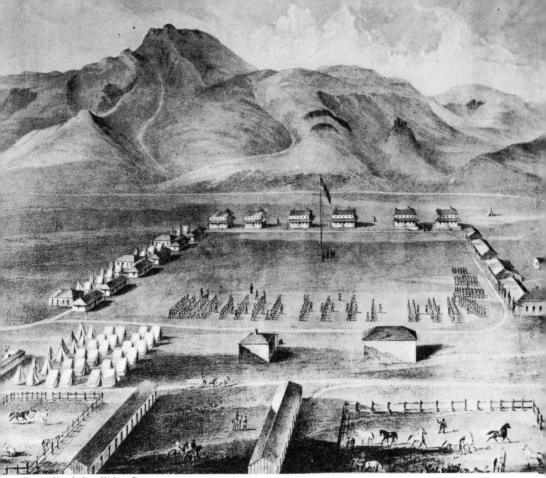

FORT CHURCHILL ON THE CARSON RIVER.

sioner of Indian Affairs there is an interesting and
informative report written by John Burche, Indian
Affairs agent for the Humboldt district, to Governor Nye. Dated August 11, 1864, parts of it provide an understanding of conditions which preceded the next year's violent conflict and insight
concerning the tribes of Indians involved.

Agent Burche first pointed out that the Indians
of his district had been peaceful and quiet during

the past two years, with the exception of small disturbances and "one or two occasions last year
[when] Indians of mixed bands from Oregon and
Idaho made a descent on the frontier settlements
of this territory and succeeded in carrying off a
few head of stock, most if not all of which was
however subsequently recovered.

"The Indians (Pah Utahs)[9] of the Humboldt
river country, as stated in a former report, are the
most quiet and tractable people I have ever met
with and are easily managed when kindly and
judiciously treated. As a people they are honest,
amiable and friendly. It is a rare thing to find one
among them who will commit a theft either upon
the whites or upon one of their own people."

Explaining that the country was fast being settled and that this was threatening the Indians'
sources of food, Burche continued, "The discovery of rich and precious minerals in southwestern
Idaho has induced for the past two years a heavy
immigration thither from California and our own
Territory. The highway to the Jordan Creek,
Boise and other mining districts of Idaho lies
through Nevada and for over two hundred miles
through Humboldt Country[10] and through two
different tribes or bands of Indians — the Pah
Utahs and the Pannakes [Bannocks]. The destruction of the grass along the route by the stock of
the immigrants was a source of great dissatisfac-
tion and discontent among these Indians as the
supply of provender for their own stock, large
numbers of which they possess, being cut off, they

STURDY T-BAR POSTS MADE OF RAILROAD RAILS MARK THE APPLEGATE-
LASSEN TRAIL AND NOBLES' ROAD ACROSS THE DESERT.
Designed and fabricated by the Nevada Trail Marking Committee, Inc., each marker bears
an inscribed brass plate. Placing the trail markers and anchoring them in cement was done
by Trails West, Inc., an organization of Nevada, California, and Oregon trail history buffs.
The trailers and campers in background are parked near Great Boiling Springs, named by
Fremont.

were compelled to seek other more distant and
less eligible localities for pasturage.

"Apprehending that trouble or disturbance
might arise between some of the bands of Indians
and the migration to Idaho from the cause of their
country being made a highway, I called together
in council in the month of May 1863, the principal
men of the Pah Ute Nation. Among them, and

most important of all, was old Wannemucka,
[Winnemucca] the head Chief of the tribe, who
was there, and had been a dweller among the
Humboldt bands since the murder of his favorite
brother Wah-he on Walker River in the previous
May by Joa-quin an Indian of the same tribe. I
stated to them that there would be a large number
of White people passing through their country up
the Humboldt River to the mountain known as
Pah-Ute Knob, thence to Queen's River and on-
wards to the Boise and Snake rivers in Idaho and
that I wished them to remain perfectly quiet and
friendly to all the whites going over the route
either way as also to the coming immigration from
the States. I further desired Wannemucka to see
or to send a delegation to Pas-se-quah, the chief of
the Pannakes of Nevada and Idaho with whom
Wannemuck is on the most friendly terms, and inform him that a large number of whites would
pass through the Pannaki country that year and
that I wanted him (Pas-se-quah) to keep his people
friendly and quiet. The old Chief freely and
promptly promised to comply with my wishes. . . .

"In a very brief period, perhaps three weeks
after the talk with Wannemuck and his people I
received word from him by an Indian to whom
Pas-se-quah gave a very handsome horse for bearing the message, that he Wannemuck wanted me
to meet the Indians — Pah Utes and Pannakes —
in Queen River Valley about seventy miles north
of Pah Ute Knob Mountain on the Humboldt. I
did so and alone. After a 'heap good talk' with
them, the Pannake Chief promised me that he

would keep his people friendly and quiet — that if no aggressive act was committed upon them by the whites that no depredation or injury should occur on the part of the Indians. I then told Pas-se-quah that a great many immigrants had been killed by his people the previous years between the Goose Creek Mountains from which the Humboldt takes its rise and the Big Bend of the river near the Pah Ute boundary line, and a large number of very valuable horses and mules stolen and run off into their country, and that I wanted him to keep his people from doing similar acts hereafter. He readily promised me that like acts should not again occur and to insure it he would not permit his people to range the river course that year during the season of immigration. It affords me the sincere satisfaction to inform Your Excellency that the Pannake chief has fulfilled his promise to the letter — No single murder, theft or other depredation has been committed by his band since within the territory to my knowledge. . . .

"Early this season by the order of Brig. Genl. Right Commanding Department of the Pacific, and at your accommodation a full company of cavalry from Fort Churchill, under the command of Capt. Wells, passed leisurely through the country into southern Idaho, thence westerly along the boundary line of Idaho, Nevada and Oregon to Goose Lake country in Oregon and then south to Susanville in California for the purpose of intimidating or suppressing any hostile intention on the part of the various bands of Indians that inhabit that line of territory. After remaining two or

three weeks in Honey Lake Valley recruiting their
horses the troop returned to Fort Churchill. It was
the first time that soldiers, for whom all the Indians have an unconcealed fear and dread, have
ever passed through this or that section of country. I doubt not that the visit of this company to
their Indian country will have a good and salutary
effect, for it is only necessary now to tell them that
if they commit any depredation or other improper
act that the soldiers will be sent for, to completely
subdue and frighten them. . . .

"I have been asked by Mr. Lockhart the Agent
of the Territory, to give the number or an approximate estimate of the number of Indians of this
division. Where the bands are always on the move,
never having a fixed location or settlement, such
an estimate is very difficult and would be necessar-
ily inaccurate, but from close personal observation
and an intimate association with the Pah Utes of
the Humboldt region for the last three years, I
should not estimate their number any below 2000
souls. As regards the Pannekes, whose range of
country extends from the Sierra to the Rocky
Mountains and from parallels 41° to 45° degrees
north latitude I cannot speak with as much certainty. They never continue in any one locality
long at a time, but rove and roam at pleasure over
all their country. I think, however, I am safe at
estimating the number that constantly or generally
range within the limits of this Territory at from
two to three thousand souls — They are by far the
most powerful and warlike tribe that dwell be-

tween the Rocky Mountains and the Pacific. They are generally well armed and equipped and possess large herds of the best horses of this section of the country, large numbers of which having been plundered from the emigrants from the States to California and Oregon and from which their own breed has been greatly improved. Many of the horses which they capture from the emigrants are superior and very valuable animals and would command very large prices in the California market for breeding and other purposes.

"In arms and ammunition they are well supplied and in the use of which they are extremely expert, economical and careful — never uselessly expending a single charge. In the season of the imigration of 1862, to my knowledge, they did not capture less than eighty or one hundred fire arms, mostly rifles and a large amount of ammunition from the unwary emigrants.

"To this tribe most of the surrounding bands are tributary or submissive — at least the Shoshones, the Pau Ut-ahs, the Pitt rivers and the Modocs are, and live in perpetual dread and fear of them. . . ."

When Indian Agent Burche wrote his 1864 report, he, of course could not foresee that anthropologists of the future would determine that the Bannocks (Pannakes) were really Northern Paiutes (Pah-utes). The language of the Bannock was identical to that of the Paiute.

In explaining his view of the origin of the Bannock, Dr. Omer C. Stewart[11] writes, "The early horse-users among the Northern Paiute of Oregon and western Idaho joined the mounted Shoshoni of Idaho and Wyoming into a mobile class which traveled from the buffalo plains to the salmon fisheries and north to hunt elk. Their poor relatives, horseless foot Shoshoni and Northern Paiute, remained in their traditional areas. . . ."

The horse-mounted Indians which Peter Skene Ogden reported near Humboldt Lake in 1829 could have been horse-using Northern Paiutes which were later named Bannocks. Observers of the 1860 Pyramid Lake battles commented on the excellent horsemanship of the Paiutes.* Many questions, including the use of horses by northwestern Nevada Indians, are more easily answered when the relationship between the Northern Paiute and the Bannock is understood.

The Indians which Burche claimed were submissive to the Bannocks must have been small, horseless bands scattered throughout the Humboldt country — a large area which was also roamed by mixed bands of Bannock-Paiute, Shoshoni, and Pitt River Indians who had horses and had broken away from the control of tribal leaders. It would be these Indians who would terrorize northern Nevada the following year.

Author's note: It is interesting to note that early Nevada ranchers recognized the Paiute Indian's ability to handle horses. Former Fernley, Nevada, rancher, J. R. ("Dick") McCulloch, was widely known for his thoroughbreds, racehorses, polo ponies, and U.S. Cavalry remounts, which he raised from about 1915 for almost a quarter of a century. His daughter and son-in-law, Betty and Dave Jackson, recently verified an old story that McCulloch used only Paiute buckaroos to break and train his horses.

FAMED NEVADA RACE HORSE, WASHOE QUEEN, AND HER PAIUTE INDIAN
TRAINER, LEVI FRASER *(left)*.
Nevada rancher Harry Drackert, who owned Washoe Queen, believes that an Indian's pa-
tience is a factor in his success as a horse trainer. But he adds, "Horses just seem to like
Indians better than other people."

Trouble along the Black Rock-Smoke Creek section of the Honey Lake-Humboldt road began
early in the year. An expressman was killed while
traveling north of Smoke Creek; and on March 1
the body of Lucius Arcularius, one of the owners
of the Granite Creek station, was found along the
road near Wall Springs. Soon after these two
murders Henry G. Blasdel, the first governor of
the new state of Nevada, began receiving worried
messages predicting an Indian outbreak which

would threaten travel across the desert to the Humboldt and Idaho mining districts.

It was shortly after dawn on March 14, 1865, in the Winnemucca Lake Valley just south of the Black Rock basin, that the Desert's Indian war was ignited. According to his military report,[12] Captain Almond B. Wells, with a detachment of fifty men of Company D, First Cavalry, Nevada Volunteers, arrived at Pyramid Lake at six o'clock on the evening of March 13.

"Immediately upon my arrival, I learned from good authority that the Indians who had been stealing cattle, and were continually making depredations among the ranchmen and settlers thereabouts were of the Smoke Creek tribe, and that a band of them was encamped about eleven (11) miles further on.[13] I placed a strict guard over a few apparently friendly Indians who had been prowling around my camp to prevent communication during the night with those below, and at three o'clock, the next morning, (the 14th inst.) I started for their encampment, taking with me twenty nine (29) men, and two citizens, who volunteered their services as guides: the balance of the command still acting as guard over those arrested the night before. At 5½ o'clock a.m. I came within sight of the encampment, halted, and dividing my men into three squads, Sergeant Wadleigh having command of one, sergeant Besat of another, and ten (10) men remaining with me. I rode on towards their camp with the purpose of arresting and taking prisoners those among them who had been guilty of cattle stealing and various other crimes. But, when within one hundred and fifty yards, they commenced firing upon me. The first shot took affect in Corporal Dolan's shoulder, wounding him slightly; the third shot passed through the cape of my overcoat. I then ordered a charge with sabers, driving the Indians back to the bushes on each side of the slough. By this time, the men under Sergeant Wadleigh and Besat came up and a general engagement ensued. The Indians fought desperately, using their guns as clubs in hand to hand conflict with my men. I followed them for about ten (10) miles up into the mountains, killing twenty nine (29) in all, but one escaped. Some old muskets, a quantity of ammunition, provisions, etc. were destroyed. I also captured nine horses but they were in too poor a condition to bring in. I was highly pleased with the conduct of my men, they were as cool and collected as though on an ordinary sabre drill. Too much praise cannot be awarded them."

In March of 1865 there were still people and a few newspapers who opposed indiscriminate killing of Indians. To some of them, Captain Well's account of the battle seemed difficult to believe, especially how twenty-nine Indians who "fought desperately" had only slightly wounded one soldier.

The Virginia City *Daily Union* newspaper reported on a meeting on March 23 between Governor Blasdel and "twenty five or thirty Chiefs and Captains" of the Paiutes. During the conference the highly respected Young Winnemucca (Numaga) stated that the camp was taken by surprise and among the dead were sixteen to eighteen women and children. He said that the men who stole the cattle were not in the camp at the time of the attack.

The *Daily Union's* report was immediately challenged by the *Territorial Enterprise* newspaper, and a heated debate, which included sardonic editorializing, began.

The *Gold Hill News*, apparently supporting the *Daily Union*, wrote in part, "This story, being still further boiled down, amounts to just this: Capt. Wells with his twenty-nine men killed exactly twenty-nine Indians, not one of the bold cavaliers having received a scratch (except Corporal Dolan, who, for thus marring the symmetry of the story, should be drummed out of the service).

"The glory of the victory is further enhanced by the announcement that "The Indians fought like veterans." The result would seem to establish the fact that they had fought about like surviving "veterans" of the revolutionary war, and with guns plowed up from the battleground of Bunker Hill. Veterans blind and palsied with age, and armed with Queen Anne's muskets, destitute of lock, stock or barrel, would have been about as formidable as these twenty-nine Paiutes seem to have been. . . ." His men were "cool and collected" — a fact which malicious traducers might attribute equally to the chilliness of the atmosphere and the total absence of the slightest danger. Well; the glorious twenty-nine have achieved glory enough for a lifetime. Their brows are bound round with victorious wreaths; their bruised arms hung up for

muskets, a quantity of Ammunition, provisions, &c: were destroyed. I also Captured nine horses, but they were in too poor a Condition to bring in. I was highly pleased with the Conduct of my men, they were as Cool and Collected as though on an ordinary Sabre drill. Too much praise Cannot be awarded them.

After all was over, Winnemucca, chief of the Py-utes, Called on me, and expressed much Satisfaction at the result of the fight. He said he had been talking to them all winter, had often warned them of the Consequences of Stealing the white men's Cattle, and now thought that the punishment they had just received was richly merited and would teach all the tribe, thievishly disposed, a permanent lesson.

Lieut. C. T. Sherwood.
Act'g Ass't Adj't Gen'l
Fort Churchill.
Nevada

I am Sir,
Very Respectfully
Your Obedient Servant

J. B. Wee
Captain, Co. "D" 1st Cav. Nev. Vol.

THE LAST PAGE OF CAPTAIN WELL'S OFFICIAL REPORT OF THE WINNEMUCCA LAKE BATTLE.
Except for Captain Well's signature, the handwriting appears to be that of Lieutenant Sherwood.

monuments, and they caper nimbly in the lager beer cellar to the lascivious pleasing of the hurdy-gurdy."

Later the *Daily Union* published a lengthly, serious review of the conflicting testimonies and rumors, concluding it with the statement, "Now, those are stories that need looking into, and after so much has been said, not half of which has been published, there is only one way in which this affair can be settled to the credit or discredit of Capt. Wells and that is by the Governor, and Major McDermit giving it a thorough investigation, which we shall insist upon until it is had."

On the basis that the Indians had fired first, Major McDermitt must have upheld Captain Wells' actions.[14] But it is doubtful that, in his first major engagement, Captain Wells covered himself with glory.

A search for personal information on Almond B. Wells has been largely unsuccessful. He was from New York. In 1865 he was twenty-three years old, and, judging by his use of the English language in his military reports, he was well educated. The "Historical Register and Dictionary of the United States Army" shows that he became a first lieutenant, Nevada Volunteer Cavalry in July of 1863. Honorably mustered out in November 1865, he returned to the service in July 1866 and thirty-five years later, in 1901, was a colonel in the First Cavalry. On April 15, 1865, a Unionville *Humboldt Register* newspaper reporter wrote:

"Captain Wells, with 108 mounted men, arrived here Wednesday afternoon, on their way to Paradise Valley — where he will rendevouz for a while, taking care of the thieving Indians in the surrounding country. Wells is a clever fellow, seeming quite civilized. Had no Indian scalps at his belt — didn't even have a large tanned scalp, with the 'dander' well up, which we expected him to bring from Virginia. Didn't give any savage war whoop as he landed but put his boys through a bit of circus performance, by talking square english to them, and then quit them, and took a smile with sundry civilians, much the same as a bloodless militia captain in the States would have done. The *Virginia Union* [*Daily Union* newspaper] has made a mistake in Wells: He is a very modest, civil fellow — and we wouldn't be afraid to go on a fishing excursion in his neighborhood.

"The soldiers are a fine-looking company and the best armed of any on this coast; having the customary carbine and saber, and in addition almost every man is supplied with one of Colt's army revolvers. They behaved well while here — no complaint whatever could be heard from them. Before cooking their supper, almost every man took a bath in the creek. 'Cleanliness is akin to godliness' — and we don't believe these fellows will disturb any godly sort of Indian."

On March 25 the *Humboldt Register* noted a condition which would be considered ominous to people who knew the ways of Indians. Stating that Major McDermit was intending to establish a

cavalry post in or near Paradise Valley, from
where in a few hours mounted men could reach
any point in the Humboldt country likely to be attacked by renegade Indians from the Black Rock
country, the article went on to say, "Some alarm
was occasioned, the other day, by the discovery
that the squaws and young piutes had been removed from the canyons. . . ."

Late in March an Indian was shot and killed by
a transient at the Granite Creek station. On the
first of April revenge swept down on three occup-
ants of the station; the mutilated bodies of two of
the white men and the burned remnants of the
third indicated the hatred the Indians had
brought with them.[15]

The Granite Creek massacre was quickly followed by a raid on Paradise Valley which brought
death to two ranchers and a heavy loss of cattle
and horses. It was a type of warfare which soon
spread across the northern part of Nevada, bring-
ing terror and loss of life and property to settlers
and travelers.

The records are not entirely clear or complete,
but available sources indicate that the most active
band of raiders across the western half of the
northern part of the state was led by an Indian
known to the whites as either Black Rock Tom or
Captain Tom. Although he moved widely and
quickly over a large area, which included Paradise
Valley and all the country through which the
roads from Honey Lake to Idaho passed, there is
little doubt that his main stronghold was in the
Black Rock Desert.

In many ways the big playa and its mountains afforded a suitable refuge for the renegade bands. Cut deep into some of the surrounding mountains are winding canyons, some of which are almost inaccessible except through narrow passages between massive rock walls. Small streams and springs in the canyons provided campsites and meadows where horses and stolen cattle could graze. From ridges which jut out above the desert, a sentinel could watch the dust of a freight wagon or cavalry column many miles distant.

Black Rock Tom's band was easily identified. The *Humboldt Register* wrote, "All hunters of Indians who came to an engagement anywhere between this and Owyhee, and almost all parties attacked on that road, during the past season, remarked a white horse of extraordinary qualities, the rider of which seemed to take great pride in his efforts to 'witch the world with noble horsemanship.' The white horse was ever spoken of as a wonder of strength and fleetness. His rider, a stalwart Indian, delighted to dally just out of musket range, caracoling most provokingly, and darting off occasionally, with the fleetness of the wind. The rider was 'Black Rock Tom'."

Late in March 1865, McDermit, realizing that a major Indian uprising was threatening, began sending troops into the Humboldt country. Lieutenant Wolverton and forty-seven men of Company D Nevada Cavalry, arrived in Star City about the first of April and were fighting Indians within the week in the Paradise Valley area.

Less than two weeks later Captain Wells with

over 100 men of Companies D and E, Nevada Cavalry, reached Unionville, and the *Humboldt Register* reported, "Capt. Wells will have, when he gets them together, 155 men. His headquarters will be at Paradise Valley — from which point he will be able to watch over that section, now rapidly settling, and protect settlers and teamsters on the Honey Lake road. A part of his force will pursue, with all haste, the band of Indians which has gone towards Black Rock with a band of stock numbering near a thousand head, horses and cattle."

During the next few months the war went badly for the Nevada troops. East of Surprise Valley, Lieutenant Littlefield engaged a large band of Indians and, finding his command outnumbered, was forced to withdraw. This defeat was soon followed by a more decisive one in the Tuscarora Range when Captain Wells, with approximately seventy men, fought a four-hour battle against a superior, fortified force which ended in retreat of the cavalry.

The *Humboldt Register* showed its concern for these setbacks. "A few more retreats, and Indian-hunting will be conducted with white people in the lead — Indians pursuing. It is unfortunate. Captain Wells undoubtedly did just what he thought was necessary. The necessity was a great misfortune — we pray it may not prove a calamity — to our people."

During the last of May, pleas from Colonel McDermit[16] and Governor Blasdel to General McDowell, commanding the Department of the Pacific, brought companies of California cavalry

REMAINS OF THE GRANITE CREEK STATION WHICH LATER BE-
CAME CAMP McKEE CAN BE SEEN ON A RANCH ALONG STATE
HIGHWAY 34, APPROXIMATELY FIVE MILES NORTH OF GER-
LACH.

and infantry into Nevada to be placed under the command of Colonel McDermit.

Four handwritten field reports by McDermit[17] tell of the remarkable attempt he made during June and July to crush the Indian war in northern Nevada. On May 30, accompanied as far as Austin by Governor Blasdel, he started on a expedition which, in regard to numbers of men involved, distances covered, and ineffectiveness in defeating the Indian forces, seems almost incredible.

Leaving Austin on June 4, McDermit traveled northward through mountainous country where ranches and dwellings were deserted because of the Indian threat. Intersecting the Humboldt River seventy miles from Unionville, he had begun to meet and collect into his command other companies of cavalry and mounted infantry already in the field. By June 12, when Captain Wells arrived, the total force had increased to over 400 men.

Near the Table Mountain area where Captain Wells had been defeated, Colonel McDermit divided his force into four commands. One unit would patrol the Humboldt and Reese rivers, another was ordered to the Queen's River, and the remaining troops were split into two groups which, from different directions, would converge at the headwaters of the Humboldt River where McDermit expected to "find the main body of Indians."

The reports show that this major military campaign actually did not succeed in engaging any large group of hostile Indians. On July 18 McDermit returned to the Little Humboldt and, after obtaining rations, proceeded with 120 cavalry and Company D, Sixth California Infantry to Queen's River Valley where a party of travelers to Boise had been attacked. Two minor engagements occurred there in which seventeen Indians were killed, making a total of forty-nine for the entire campaign.

On the final page of McDermit's August 2 report (which may have been his last written communication) he wrote, "We then struck the trail of the main party of Indians who were engaged in the fight against Cap Wells on the 20th of May and whom we previously followed from the State

BAND OF THE THIRD INFANTRY, CALIFORNIA VOLUNTEERS.

of Nevada to Idaho Territory. We followed this trail to the point where they attacked the party of citizens en route to the Boise Mines on the 3rd of July last. From this point they have directed their course toward the white or Snow Mountains in Oregon. As soon as I rest my cavalry horses and have some shoeing done I will continue following them. I have now followed these Indians from Nev to Idaho Territory thence into Utah Territory. I then returned to Nevada and again followed them into the Oyhee in Idaho. Now I shall pursue them to Oregon."

But Colonel McDermit did not go to Oregon. The kindly man, who did not believe in indiscriminate killing of Indians, was fatally wounded in an ambush near Queen's River and died on August 7.

During the summer months Nevada and Idaho newspapers had become increasingly pessimistic about the condition of the conflict. Boise's *Idaho Tri-Weekly Statesman* newspaper of June 24, announcing the arrival of the Humboldt Express stage from California and Nevada, wrote, "The messenger says he was compelled to run the gauntlet of about 200 miles of hostile savages. . . . All of the stations have been abandoned and the settlers have left the country. . . . This is the last time the Express will be brought that way until there is more certainty of getting through alive. . . . It is useless to ignore the fact that there must be some good fighting done on an extensive scale or the whole country from the Owyhee River to California and Nevada must be abandoned to the Indians."

The inability of the military to defeat the Indian bands decisively is understandable. The cavalry was in unfamiliar country, engaged in a type of fighting in which they were inexperienced. Conversely, the bands of Indian raiders knew every canyon and spring and could usually move quickly out of reach of troops — or, if they so wished, choose the most advantageous battleground. The relatively small number of cavalry units could not cover the large area from which urgent demands for protection were constantly pouring into Fort

Churchill. For instance, on July 3 E. D. Pierce wrote Colonel McDermit requesting a military post in Soldier Meadows to protect the new Chico,

Courtesy Robert Amesbury

MR. E. D. PIERCE OPERATED THE CHICO, CALIFORNIA TO RUBY CITY, IDAHO STAGE LINE WHICH TRAVELED THROUGH THE BLACK ROCK DESERT IN 1865.

California, to Ruby City, Idaho, stage road which turned north from the Humboldt road at Granite Creek to pass through Soldier Meadows to Summit Lake, Pueblo, Jordan Creek Valley, and into southwestern Idaho. After pointing out that he must have protection to carry the mail, Pierce added a postscript to his handwritten letter[18] which provides an eyewitness account of an event often mentioned in books on Nevada history. Mr. Pierce's spelling was far from accurate, but his report should be authentic.

"P. S. We hade a sade axcident that accurde June 24th. Campt at the Soldjers Medows over Nite and the Next Mornin when we was prepearing to starte theare was a few harsh wordes that took place betwene Wm Reagean and Bearnehearte in reffernce to a Roap that belonged to Reagean. Bearnehearte struck Reagean and at the same time plaste his hand on his Pistol. Reagean told him not to draw it and stooped down and got holte of a small rock and thrue it and hit Bearnehearte on the arm. Bearnehearte drew his Pistol and fierd three shots the first with no effect the second past throughe his left Rist the third entered his left Brest and he Reagean fell dead. We was 40 in number who after cam and delibereate reflection gave Bearnehearte fear and imprearciel triel founde him giltey of Murder in the first degree and hung him. Thus it is Mans days ar few and full of trubel hope to heare from you soon. E. D. P."

DENIO TO WINNEMUCCA FREIGHT TEAM, 1868.

To protect the road, a military post was established at remote Summit Lake.

The old records show that the tide of war began to change during the first part of September and that the change was partly due to the ability of a Paiute Indian named Captain Sou.

During August, with raids continuing, white residents of northern Nevada were showing increased hatred of even friendly Indians. Captain Sou, leader of Unionville's colony of Paiutes, sensed the growing feeling with apprehension that the actions of the renegade bands would eventually destroy all the state's Indian people. Knowing that the military needed Indian scouts who knew both the country and the enemy, Sou offered his services to the cavalry.

During September, with Captain Sou and several other scouts from his tribe guiding the troops, two Indian bands were surprised and badly defeated. But it was not until mid-November that a major battle began to clear northern Nevada's most dangerous raiders from their Black Rock Desert stronghold.

On November 4, an Indian war party attacked a freight wagon along the road between the desert and the Humboldt River. The driver was mutilated and killed and the wagon burned.

When news of the raid reached Dun Glen, Lieutenant Penwell and twenty-six men, with Captain Sou as guide, started for the area where the attack had occurred. After examining the scene of the murder and determining that Black Rock Tom's band had been responsible, Sou led the cavalry north along the east side of the Black Rock Range.

Accounts state that the raiders were found intrenched in the mountains west of Paiute Meadows. Paiute Creek flows through a deep narrow mountain canyon onto the meadows, and it is probable that the Indians were waiting where steep rock walls jut from both sides of the canyon to create a natural, formidable fortress.

Lieutenant Penwell made an attempt to dislodge the Indians but soon found it was impossible with

DUN GLEN WAS A MINING CAMP WHEN A MILITARY POST WAS ESTABLISHED THERE.

his small force. Without casualties on either side, the cavalry turned back for Dun Glen.

On November 13, Lieutenant R. A. Osmer, Second Cavalry, California Volunteers, set out with a larger number of men and better equipment in an attempt to bring final defeat to Black Rock Tom. His handwritten offical report[19] is interesting and probably more accurate than the somewhat more dramatic version published in the *Humboldt Register* newspaper.

Sir: I have the honor to report that in compliance with Post Orders No. 35 dated HdQrs. Dun Glen Nov. 12th, 1865, I left Post at 8:30 A.M.

on the 13th inst. with 60 enlisted men of Co. B 2 Cav. C.V., and one Mountain Howitzer; also three citizens of Dun Glen joined my command, and we proceeded to scout the country in the vicinity of the Black Rock Mountains. Marched that day to St. Mary's — distance 18 miles. Broke camp next morning at daybreak and marched to Willow Creek Station — distance 18 miles — when 7 enlisted men joined company. At this point we were also joined by ten Indian warriors under Captain "Sou", the chief of the band of friendly "Piutes" at Big Meadows. I had sent an express for these warriors to join my command at this station for guides as well as to fight; also one white man named Swim who is well acquainted with the country and was of the greatest service as a guide. Broke camp on the 15th inst. at daybreak and marched to Dunshea Springs — distance 35 miles. No grass and but little water and sagebrush. Broke camp on the 16th at daybreak, and marched to Jackson's Ranch — distance 25 miles, plenty of wood and water and but little grass. Broke camp on the 17th at two o'clock A.M. and marched 30 miles in a northwesterly direction, attacking the Indian Camp at Sunrise of the same morning. The fight lasted about two and a half hours, and extended over a space about 6 miles square. Until one of my command was killed but few squaws had been slain, and those by mistake, as it was impossible to distinguish one from another — nothing but a head peeping over a rock or a sagebrush — and I had given orders that no squaws should be killed, but at this time the rage of my Indian allies, and

IT IS BELIEVED THAT BLACK ROCK TOM'S BAND WAS EN-
TRENCHED BEHIND THIS NATURAL FORTRESS IN PAIUTE
CREEK CANYON.

men also, could not be controlled. About 120 Indians in all were killed, of which 80 were "Bucks",
and I do not know of but one Indian escaping.
These Indians are "Bannocks",[20] and the same
who killed and robbed the teamster 35 miles from
this Post, about two weeks ago, as we found fine
clothing, tobacco, new blankets, etc., with which

his teams were loaded. We destroyed a large lot of provisions, 22 "Campoodies," and everything that could not be taken off. We captured a quantity of ammunition, several guns, 5 Indian ponies and some blankets; our loss was Private David W. O'Connell, killed, 1 Sergeant and 1 Private wounded, also one horse wounded. I also lost 4 Privates, 5 horses and their arms and accoutrements by desertion, on the 14th inst. I left the Indian camp at 12 M. on the 17th inst. and arrived back at Jackson's Ranch at dark, distance marched 30 miles and about 15 miles marched during the fight. Broke camp at daybreak on the 18th, and marched to Dunshea Springs, distance 25 miles. Broke camp at daybreak on the 19th and marched to St. Mary's, distance 36 miles. Broke camp at 2 o'clock A.M. on the 20th and arrived at Dun Glen at 6 o'clock A.M., distance 18 miles, having been out 7 days and marched about 250 miles.

Very Respectfully,
Your Ob'dt Serv't
R. A. Osmer
1st Lieut. 2nd Cavalry, C.V.
Commanding Post

The Thompson and West's 1881 *History of Nevada* states, "Only six Indians and five squaws escaped, among whom was Black Rock Tom."

That the leader did escape is made certain by a letter from Lieutenant Osmer to Fort Churchill, dated December 18, 1865.[21]

"Sir: I have this day recd a letter from Thomas

FROM ABOVE THE PAIUTE CANYON FORTRESS, CRAIG STUDIES
ANGLES FOR HIS PAINTING.

Stark, a citizen living on the Humboldt River, at
Smith's Crossing, who informs me that Capt Tom
and two of his tribe of Indians, the same that I
had the fight with on the 17th of November, 1865,
have come to his place and surrendered themselves to him and sued for peace, and want to
form some treaty. I have asked him to keep the
Indians until I could hear from headquarters District of Nevada. I have talked with Captain Sou,
who is a friendly Indian and was out with me in
the fight. He says Captain Tom is a very bad Indian and will not keep peace long. The inhabitants

in the vicinity say he is one of the worst Indians in the country. I would respectfully ask if I shall take any notice of the communication."

On December 30 the *Humboldt Register* reported: "Several messengers have come, lately, from Capt. Sou to citizens here, asking them to come down to the Big Meadows and be put in the possession of the notorious cut-throat known as 'Black Rock Tom'. Those who have been accustomed to attend to such business were busy, and Tom remained on the Meadows, doubtless feeling each day more secure. When Capt. Street came that

PAIUTE CREEK CANYON OFFERED THE INDIANS EXCELLENT TERRAIN FOR AMBUSH OR DEFENSE.

way, Tuesday, Sou notified him of the opportunity to capture this leading marauder. Street took him in charge and gave him in keeping to a squad of his boys, with particular instruction not to permit an escape. Soon after Tom attempted to escape and several musket balls blew through his chest in an instant. Tom will murder no more travelers."

Another article in the same paper of that date included: "He has quit this vale of tears; but the horse has not been taken. Tom did not bring the pale horse on his last trip, and so the noble and much-coveted animal is still in Indian hands."

The final battle, which removed the last large band of Indian raiders from their Black Rock Desert stronghold, was fought on January 12, 1866. The official report concerning the fight consists of only seven lines of handwriting. Fortunately, the *Humboldt Register* devoted most of its front page of January 20 to the expedition, and thus preserved one of the Black Rock Desert's most dramatic stories.

A GALLANT FIGHT IN FISH CREEK VALLEY

"One of the best fights yet recorded since the Indians of our northern border commenced hostilities, was made near the confluence of Queen's River and Fish Creek* last week. We give a some-

---

Author's note: An extensive search of the maps compiled in the 1860s has not located a stream named Fish Creek in the vicinity of Queen's River. This is understandable because the maps show many changes, for example Queen's to Quinn River and Antelope to Jackson Mountains. The distances and directions given in the newspaper and in two military reports place Fish Creek in the northern end of the Black Rock Desert where three streams —

what extended and correct account of the expedition as being a remarkable triumph over terrible hardships incident to bad weather, and as being more interesting to our readers than any other matter with which the account might be replaced. The gallant officer who had charge of the campaign — the brave soldiers who sprang like electric sparks from the chrysalis state into which the ice was reducing them when the order 'forward' was given — the gallant citizens, who gave up the ease and comfort of town life to hunt the common enemy — and even The Piutes, who attest their friendship by secretly guiding the white man to the enemy's camps — all earned our gratitude.

"The Indians had become so daring and troublesome, of late, that communication between Dun Glen and Camp McDermit was unsafe. The Queen's river region was dangerous. (Is yet, for that matter.) Capt. G. D. Conrad, of Company B, Second Cal. Vol. Cavalry, determined on a raid against the marauders. The campaign having been planned and all preparations made, the command set out from Dun Glen on the morning of the 8th, headed for Queen's river. The force was composed as follows: Of Co. B, 35 men; citizens, 9; Piutes, 12. We have been furnished by Mr. W. K. Parkinson, of the expedition, the particulars as they transpired — substantially as follows:

"Night of the 9th, camped at Willow Point Sta-

Leonard, Bartlett and Battle Creeks — once flowed into the Queen's River. In agreement with Mitchell and Jim Bidart of the Leonard Creek Ranch, it is believed that Leonard Creek was called Fish Creek in 1865, and that Battle Creek received its name from the January 12, 1866, fight.

tion, Paradise Valley. Remained there until the
evening of the 10th, and made a night march over
the mountains into the Queen's river Valley, in
order to enter the Valley unobserved; and camped
at Cane Springs. Capt. Conrad, Thos. Ewing, and
Sergeant Korble, having gone ahead during the
day and ascended a high Mountain Peak, commanding a view of the Valley of Queen's river,
kept a sharp lookout for fires until 9 o'clock at
night; and no fires appearing, the Captain cor-
rectly concluded that the Indians had left the valley — the weather being so very cold that fire was
a necessity. During the night the command was
joined by a detachment of 25 men from Company
I, same regiment, commanded by Lieut. Duncan
accompanied by Dr. Snow, a citizen physician.

"On the morning of the 11th, it having snowed
during the night, and the morning being very cold
and stormy, the snow blowing in clouds, the command was in motion as soon as it was light enough
to see, marching towards Queen's river, 20 miles
distant. Reached the river in the afternoon, and
after much difficulty found a deep hole in the
river that was not frozen solid, and cut through
the ice and camped. The water was so full of sulphur and decayed matter that the horses would
not drink it, and the men were compelled to melt
the ice to get water with which to make coffee.
That night Capt. Conrad, with four soldiers, Parkinson, Ewing, and Indians Sou and Bob, went on
a scout; and after a cold and difficult ride of 7
miles in a westerly direction from the camp, they
reached the summit of a range of mountains lying

"...THE MORNING BEING VERY COLD AND STORMY, THE SNOW BLOWING IN CLOUDS, THE COMMAND WAS IN MOTION AS SOON AS IT WAS LIGHT ENOUGH TO SEE, MARCHING TOWARDS QUEEN'S RIVER, 20 MILES DISTANT."

between Queen's river Valley and Fish creek Valley, from which point they had a view of Fish creek Valley for thirty miles. They discovered fires in a northwesterly direction, and on the further side of Fish creek Valley — as nearly as they could determine, about 12 miles from the base of the mountain on which they stood. Capt. Sou thought from the appearance of the fires that there were a great many warriors, and that the command would have a hard fight. The Captain took bearings and directions as well as could be done under the circumstances, and determined to make the attack at daylight on the following morning. The scouting party returned to camp, and the order was given for the command to be in the saddle at half-past 11 o'clock. The brave boys in blue received the announcement with joy. Then followed the bustle and preparation for battle: supper at 10 o'clock; horses fed; extra ammunition issued; pack train and wagons ordered to follow at daylight.

THE NIGHT MARCH

"Precisely at half-past 11 o'clock the order to march was given, and the entire command formed in line. Capt. Conrad gave the necessary orders, forbidding indiscriminate slaughter of women and children, and the command commenced the long, cold march of 20 miles. The night was dark and stormy. Having to cross Fish creek, and there being many hot springs along that stream, making it miry in the coldest weather, an early start was necessary, in order to make some allowances for delay if any occurred. Weather intensely cold. Not a word spoken. No sound but the dull tramp of the horses through the snow. Marched without hindrance until 3 o'clock a.m., when column halted and was ordered to dismount. Supposed to be as near the Indians as we dare approach until daylight. No Indian fires to be seen. Cold increasing. Men actually freezing.

A CIRCUS, WHERE ALL PERFORM. — ADMISSION FREE–ZING.

"Not daring to approach nearer the watchful enemy, for fear of alarming him before we could

see to properly dispose of him; and the cold stead-
ily gaining in its effects upon the men; it became
painfully certain that something must be done, to
keep human blood in condition for a boil — the
time for which was so near at hand. The men
made circles about the size of circus rings, and ran
in them to keep warm. It was a curious scene, in
the center of that snowy desert, a company of 80
men, on that terrible night, running around in circles as if running for their lives. All running —
Captain, Piutes, and all; and this performance
continued actively for 3 long hours. Even with this
extraordinary effort to save themselves, over 20
men were frozen — their hands, feet, or faces.
Notwithstanding all they suffered, not a murmur
of complaint was uttered by the soldiers. The
horses huddled up close together, and were covered with a white mantle of frost; seeming frozen
together.

DAYLIGHT

"Daylight came. The intense cold aroused the
Indians early, and immediately after daylight fires
arose about 5 miles west of the command — although it did not appear near so far. All was excitement in a moment. Capt. Conrad, cool and de-
liberate under all circumstances, ordered the men
to carefully examine their fire arms, adjust and
secure their saddles properly, and prepare for action. He then divided the command into three
columns — Lieut. Duncan, Co. I, commanding
right column, Sergeant Korble, Co. B, commanding the left, and Conrad the center. The columns

"THE MEN MADE CIRCLES ABOUT THE SIZE OF CIRCUS RINGS,
AND RAN IN THEM TO KEEP WARM. IT WAS A CURIOUS SCENE,
IN THE CENTER OF THAT SNOWY DESERT."

took their respective positions, and advanced —
with intervals of three quarters of a mile between
columns, until near the Indians, when each column was ordered into line.

THE FIGHT

"The fight commenced in all its fury. The Indian encampments were on the western side of
Fish creek Valley, about 60 miles west of Paradise
Valley — the mountains of the west forming a
half-circle around the camps, about 3½ miles distant. The Indians had the advantage of the

ground. The field fought over was about 2 miles square, and a large portion of it was covered with tules, and tall rye grass, and very much cut up with gullies and ravines; and bore also a great quantity of Spanish broom. The Indians could not have selected a field better adapted to their style of warfare. The Indians discovered the three columns coming dashing down on them when about a mile distant, and then they could be distinctly seen preparing for battle; dividing off into squads of from 4 to 6, and selecting their places for combat where it would be most difficult to maneuver cavalry. Each warrior had from 50 to 75 poisoned arrows, giving each squad from 250 to 350 shots. The moment before the battle commenced, owing to the extreme cold a dense cloud of frost commenced flying, so thick that a horseman could not be distinctly seen over 100 yards. This gave the Indians a great advantage, as it compelled the soldiers to fight at short range, so that the bow and arrow could be used; and it also increased the chances of escape for the Indians. Had the frost commenced flying earlier, no doubt many of them would have escaped. The plan of battle was such that the right and left columns flanked the Indians, and soon surrounded them. They fought with desperation. In no instance did a warrior lay down his arms till he laid down his life. They arranged their arrows between their fingers in such a manner that they could shoot them very rapidly, and charged with as much bravery as any soldiers in the world. The excitement was intense. Soldiers, citizens, and the savages, charging and yelling;

"THE MOMENT BEFORE THE BATTLE COMMENCED, OWING TO THE EXTREME COLD A DENSE CLOUD OF FROST COMMENCED FLYING, SO THICK THAT A HORSEMAN COULD NOT BE DISTINCTLY SEEN OVER 100 YARDS."

each straining all his powers to destroy the other; the wild, ringing war–whoop, the rapid firing of 80 disciplined men; the thunder of a cavalry charge; all, together, created a scene that beggars description. Capt. Conrad seemed everywhere in the fight — now leading his men in a charge, now fighting single-handed; and no peril did he not share with his men — never asking them to go where he would not lead. Lieut. Duncan behaved nobly, and is a brave and gallant soldier. Sergeant Korbel led his column into the action in the most gallant manner, striking the enemy the first blow, and continuing to fight nobly throughout the battle.

"Dr. Snow, a citizen physician accompanying the detachment from Company I, will be long remembered and loved by the gallant men who fought that day. He rode over all parts of the field during the battle, attending to the wounded soldiers where they fell, applying the antidotes necessary to destroy the deadly effect produced by poisoned arrows — which if not attended to at once must prove fatal. An old man, whose head is white with the frost of many Winters, but whose heart is as warm and his energies as vigorous as those of a youth, he braved the perils of frost and battle to alleviate the suffering of his fellow men. May God protect him, is the soldier's prayer. Many heroic deeds were performed. Each individual was a hero, and none but faced death like veterans.

"The battle continued in full force for two and a half hours, when the conflict was reduced to two points, at which several warriors had selected deep, short gullies, and were making what they knew to be their last fight. In one of these places the Captain of the Band, Capt. John, a large, powerful Indian, apparently about 35 years of age, having one man with him, was defending himself with skill; and knowing that he must die, he determined to sell his life dearly. He was a warrior of renown, having been a leader from the commencement of hostilities. He had killed Col. McDermit and a soldier by the name of Rafferty — last year. Capt. John and his comrade had each a bow and quiver, and Capt. John was using the identical rifle with which he killed McDermit. After a great deal of sharp shooting, Capt. Rapley succeeded in shooting him through the head, and Capt. John was dead.

"The battle, with the exception of a few straggling shots, was over. The Indians had fought with a heroism that astonished everyone who witnessed it. They made no offer to surrender; uttered no sound but yells of defiance; and continued to fire their poisoned arrows until they were so weak that they could throw them but a few feet; and some of them dying would shoot an arrow straight up in the air, in hope that the deadly missile would fall on the heated and victorious foe. At the close of the battle 35 dead Indians lay on the field with their bows and quivers still clutched in their hands. All were large, powerful men — a picked company of braves, prepared for battle. But 5 squaws were in the band, and they were acting in the capacity of pack train. Two of these were killed in battle by mistake; the other three were furnished with some provisions and left unmolested.

"Scouting parties made the entire circuit of the field, and found that no living thing had escaped, as the snow was 3 inches deep and there were no tracks leading from the camp. . . .

"The Indian camps all destroyed, the wounded all cared for, the command marched for Fish creek, where water could be obtained, and camped — the trains having arrived there before them. On the night of the 12th snow fell, and the morning of the 13th was blustering and stormy. At daylight

marched for Cane Springs. After the command
had started, and as the last of the pack train was
leaving camp, they saw an Indian coming on the
trail from the direction of the battle field. They
awaited his arrival, and he proved to be an Indian

BATTLE CREEK.

lad of about 15 years, who had determined to join the whites and was ready to be reconstructed. The Captain was summoned from the front, and with the aid of interpreters the boy made the following statement: He said that an old man, a young man and himself, were in the mountains the morning of the battle, and knew nothing of it until in the afternoon, when they came down to the camp. He said all the fighting men engaged in the battle were dead but 4, 3 of them being mortally wounded and the other shot through the legs. These 4 wounded men he found hidden in the tules and rye grass. He says that there are no other Indians in those mountains at this time, except those that were with him the morning of the battle. Wounded all comfortable cared for and put in wagons, and the command reached Cane Springs on the night of the 13th, Willow Point Station in Paradise Valley, the night of the 14th, and Dun Glen in the afternoon of the 15th; having made the ride from Willow Point Station to Dun Glen, 47 miles, in 7 hours."

Other smaller engagements occurred in northern Nevada during the next several years, but relative peace settled over the desert. Within months the Indian's Black Rock stronghold was crawling with white men armed with prospecting picks. Newspapers had reported that the legendary Hardin silver lode had been found.

NOTES TO CHAPTER V

1. Weatherlow's statement is contained in a letter from Colonel Frederick W. Lander to the United States commissioner of Indian Affairs.

2. The story of Hardin's lost silver lode is told in Chapter 6.

3. F. F. Kingsbury, "Peter Lassen's Pipe," unpublished (Pioneer Letters, California State Library, circa 1939).

4. F. F. Kingsbury claimed the horse was Lassen's Wild Tom.

5. F. F. Kingsbury's short sketch of Peter Lassen's life and comments about his death were typed on three pages of stationery bearing his son's letterhead, "B. C. Kingsbury, D.D.S."

6. Asa M. Fairfield, *Fairfield's Pioneer History of Lassen County, California* (H. S. Crocker Co., 1916).

7. Accounts of this important battle can be read in Thompson and West's *History of Nevada* (1881; reprint ed. Berkeley, Calif.: Howell-North Books, 1958). Also see F. Egan, *Sand in a Whirlwind* (Garden City, N.Y.: Doubleday, 1972); and S. S. Wheeler, *The Desert Lake* (Caldwell, Idaho: Caxton Printers, 1967).

8. A discussion of the tribal connections of Indians composing these "renegade" bands will follow later in this chapter in connection with Indian agent Burche's 1864 report to Governor Nye.

9. Paiutes.

10. Northern California through Honey Lake Valley, across Black Rock Desert to Lassen's Meadow, Humboldt River to present site of Winnemucca, north to Paradise Valley, to Quinn River Valley, and on to Idaho.

11. Omer C. Stewart, "The Question of Bannock Territory," in *Languages and Cultures of Western North America: Essays in Honor of Sven S. Liljeblad*, ed. Earl H. Swanson, Jr. (Pocatello: Idaho State University, 1970).

12. This official report was not written until September 21, 1865.

13. The encampment "11 miles further on" was near the south end of Winnemucca Lake, called "Mud Lake" in 1865.

14. In a 32-page military service file for Captain Wells, secured from the Navy and Old Army Branch, Military Archives Division, National Archives, there is no indication that a Court of Inquiry was held.

15. A detailed account of the Granite Creek event was originally published in the April 15, 1865, issue of Unionville's *Humboldt Register* newspaper.

16. Major McDermit had been promoted to lieutenant colonel.

17. These were included among photocopies of approximately 125 handwritten pages of 1865-66 military reports and letters obtained from the Old Military Records Division of the National Archives.

18. National Archives.

19. Ibid.

20. It would be interesting to know why Osmer believed they were Bannocks.

21. National Archives.

22. Ranchers in the area still tell a story, handed down through several generations, of a lone Indian surviving the battle and escaping by climbing the cliff over which Battle Creek falls.

CHAPTER VI

The Lost Silver Lode
and the Rock Hounds

ORDINARILY the small piece of rock would have been discarded or misplaced. But to its owner, a carpenter in Petaluma, California, it may have recalled memories of his adventures as an 1849 wagon-train scout, and he retained it in his possession for more than eight years.*

During the winter of 1857 or the spring of 1858, the rock's metallic appearance was brought to the attention of an assayer, and a bizarre chain of events was set in motion. Directly or indirectly because of the result of the assay, untold numbers of men came to the desert; one of California's most prominent pioneers lost his life under mysterious circumstances; a town and ore mills and furnaces were built for the "fabulously rich" Black Rock mines; and a confusing record, which failed to document clearly the production of a single ounce of precious metal, was left to posterity. His-

*Author's note: The following account of the lost Hardin silver lode is brief, including only the main events of the complex story. For more detail, Fairfield's *Pioneer History of Lassen County, California* is suggested. Although out of print, Fairfield's book should be available in most large public and university libraries. Asa M. Fairfield was a teacher in Honey Lake Valley schools from 1875 to 1899 and personally knew most of the early settlers or their families. While his account of the lost silver lode shows extensive newspaper research, it also contains information provided by pioneer families. He states that his story "is the way it has always been told by the men of this part of the country. . . ."

torian Asa M. Fairfield, writing in 1916, said that
he considered the story of the Black Rock mines
one of the strangest lost mine stories told on the
coast.

According to early historians, James Allen Hardin acted as scout and hunter for a wagon train
which in 1849 followed the Lassen Trail enroute
to California. By the time the party had reached
the vicinity of the Black Rock there was concern
for a dwindling food supply. Hardin, probably accompanied by another man, set out along the west
side of the Black Rock Range hoping to find
game.

Traveling through foothills several miles north
of Double Hot Springs, the hunters noticed something shining in the bottom and along the sides of
a small, water-eroded ravine. On stopping to examine the material they decided it was lead and,
because they were short of ammunition, they collected some of it and carried it with them to the
camp. There some of it was melted and formed
into musket balls.[1] Hardin kept a small piece and
had it with him when he settled in Petaluma.

The records do not reveal when or why the
metallic rock was assayed, but they do claim that it
was found to be carbonate of lead and silver, and
very rich in silver.

An expedition to the Black Rock was inevitable,
but it was not until July of 1858 that a party of
about fifteen men, led by Hardin, left for the desert. Hardin was certain he remembered the location of the ravine, but nine years had passed and
either the appearance of the area had changed or

his memory was faulty. The party searched until fall without success.

Hardin spent the winter in Petaluma and returned to the Black Rock early in 1859. Apparently this second expedition was also unsuccessful, although Hardin and his party are said to have recorded a ledge. It was during 1859 that Honey Lake Valley prospectors became more interested in the story of a rich silver deposit, and Peter Lassen made his fatal trip in an attempt to locate it.

In the spring of 1860 there were approximately eighty prospectors in the Black Rock country. When news of the start of the Pyramid Lake Indian War reached them they left the region. From 1860 to 1865 interest in the Hardin lode declined, with only a few people from nearby communities in northwestern Nevada and Honey Lake Valley periodically prospecting the area. The situation quickly changed in January 1866 when word from the desert claimed the Hardin silver ledge had been found. Soon hundreds of men were on their way to the Black Rock.

Nevada and California newspapers were largely responsible for the almost instant fame of the "discovery." The news stories, most of which were based on letters from the mines, must have been confusing to readers. Claims of a silver ledge so rich that it might "revolutionize the monetary affairs of the nation" and ore "running $2,700 to the ton" were followed by reports that assayers could find little or no silver or gold in their samples. In March the *Humboldt Register* wrote, "Black Rock is all the go now. Thursday forenoon a storm was on

. . . but it did not deter a number of prospectors from setting out for the new El Dorado. When you see a man sitting in front of a roll of blankets and a frying pan, and behind a Henry rifle, you need not ask him where he is going — he is going to Black Rock or burst."

Later in March the *Register* commented, "Those we have spoken with have no faith in the reputed richness of the ore there found. They describe the ledges as monstrous in width, and cropping from three to ten miles on the surface. If they are good silver ore, the boys say it is the heaviest deposit of it ever yet found in the world. One thing puzzles people. The assayers here [Unionville] can make out but a bare trace of silver in any of the Black Rock ores yet tried, while Isenbeck and Mosheimer [assayers at Black Rock] make certifi-

THE PLAYA, WITH ITS WIND EROSION AND STORMS, HAS AL-MOST ERADICATED THE ONCE BUSY HARDIN CITY.

ENROUTE TO HARDIN CITY.

cates of fabulous results. Black Rock is as much a
mystery as ever."

In July a Washoe City newspaper, *The Eastern
Slope*, said of the Black Rock, "Ledges of unlimited
extent pay $50 a ton from the top down and this
exceeds any discovery ever made before in the
mining world."

By August a mill was being built at Hardin City,
"a city of 15 houses and 15,000 rats"[2] and many
tents.

Throughout the remainder of the year and during 1867 the Black Rock mines situation continued
to be inexplicable. The initial rush to the area was
over, but conflicting reports continued to come
out of the desert. Two additional mills were being
built, while statements such as "$8,000 from

twenty tons of rock . . . one pound of pure silver from four pounds of rock" were being contested by an owner of the first Hardin City mill, who admitted, "I have yet to see a quarter of a dollar in silver or gold actually produced from working the Black Rock ores. . . ."

By March of 1868 the mills of the district, unable to take gold or silver from the ores, had ceased operation. Fairfield believed that the mines were abandoned by everyone by the middle of 1868.

One of the early prospectors, Ladue Vary, continued to prospect the Black Rock Range and eventually discovered a ledge containing gold and silver in a canyon on the eastern side of the mountains farther north than Hardin City. According to Fairfield he was offered $30,000 for his mine, which would have allowed him to retire, but he would not sell for less than $100,000. A buyer at that price was not found, and Vary leased out the mining rights.[3] He continued to live on his property, which became known as Varyville, and raised a garden and some hay. In 1906 he had become so feeble he was taken to the County Hospital at Winnemucca, Nevada, where he died the next year at an age of ninety-six.

Some of the old rock houses still stand at Varyville, and there are planted trees and a meadow. An old prospector probably found it a pleasant place to live.

There are legends of other lost mines in the Black Rock region, of which the Lost Blue Bucket is the most famous. Similar to the Hardin story, it

A VARYVILLE RESIDENCE.

began with a wagon train en route to California. While the party struggled through a steep and rocky canyon, the children amused themselves by tossing pebbles into buckets which dangled along the sides of some of the wagons. When the train reached Yreka, California, some of the pebbles still remained in a blue bucket. They were identified as solid gold nuggets.

A party of fifteen men returned to the Black Rock Desert the following spring but before reaching the canyon were victims of an Indian attack which left only two of them alive. Later expeditions were unsuccessful. Eventually attempts to find the canyon were abandoned in favor of the search for gold in the Sacramento Valley.

There are many good reasons for doubting the story. A widely read version contains obvious inaccuracies in geography, dates and Indian history. But a Nevada librarian recently affirmed that each summer amateur prospectors search library shelves for clues to the location of the Lost Blue Bucket Mine.

Is there a bonanza somewhere in the Black Rock Range? After talking with many men who had prospected the area and reading everything he could find, Asa M. Fairfield wrote that he believed "Mr. Hardin found the large quantity of that silver ore just as he said he did. He was not hunting for gold or silver and didn't expect to find any, and was not excited about it. He simply thought he had found something that would make bullets. Cloud-bursts are of frequent occurrence in the Black Rock region during hot weather. Men who knew that section well in the 60s and who went back there twenty-five years afterwards, say it then looked like a strange country because cloud-bursts had cut out new canyons and filled up the old ones. Probably a year or two before Hardin had found ore a cloud-burst had torn open the side of the hill and exposed it to view. Before he came back in 1858 another cloud-burst covered it up. This view was taken by M. S. Thompson, Leroy Arnold, and other men who prospected in that

IN JUNE, FROM VARYVILLE, SNOW CAN STILL BE SEEN ON THE BLACK ROCK
RANGE.

district. The next cloud-burst that comes along
may uncover it again, and, on the other hand, it
may lie buried there forever."

During a recent discussion with Director John
H. Schilling of the Nevada Bureau of Mines and
Geology, he said, "It is possible that Hardin did
find a small pocket of very rich ore which could
have been exposed by a cloudburst and then re-
buried. Small isolated concentrations of high-
grade ore are not uncommon, and sometimes,
especially in the early days, the value of a ledge
was falsely based on the assays of samples taken
from one pocket — which could have been the
only valuable ore on the property."

The old prospectors who searched for the desert's treasures are gone, but they have been replaced by a similar type of hardy individuals who also dig in the mountains of the Black Rock. If the ghost of James Allen Hardin still searches for the lost lode, it must feel less lonely in the late spring of each year when hundreds of rock hounds come to the desert.

According to D. Fred Parrish, past president of the Reno Gem and Mineral Society, the Black Rock basin is one of the West's well-known rock-hunting areas. Calling it "nature's rock-hound supermarket," Fred says an incomplete inventory would list approximately thirty-five kinds of agates, petrified woods, obsidian of various colors and shades, quartz crystals, geodes, fossils, and fire opals.

It is usually on a Friday evening preceding the Memorial Day holiday that Nevada, California, Oregon and other gem and mineral clubs raise long trails of dust as their modern wagon trains cross the desert toward the Black Rock Range. Sometimes a group stops to ask directions, and it is easy to see the excitement of those who have come to the big playa for the first time. Double Hot Springs, approximately five miles north of the Black Rock, is a favorite camping area, and by Saturday morning tents, pickup truck campers, and travel trailers cover several acres of the same ground emigrants used more than one and a quarter centuries before.

Not long after sunrise each day the rock hunters head for hillside ledges or surface collecting areas.

Fred claims that some of the older members take advantage of their age and send the young ones up the steeper slopes to explore and take samples. If something worthwhile is found, the old-timers then climb the mountain.

Roads of the Black Rock Range are rough and steep, and usually more than one car has tire, engine, transmission, or other mechanical failure. Vehicle problems are not limited to the mountain climbers; it is not uncommon for someone crossing the playa to become mired in mud.

Fred tells of a field trip when seven cars of Reno

CALIFORNIA AND OREGON ROCKHOUNDS LIKE TO CAMP AT DOUBLE HOT SPRINGS. THEY TRAVEL THERE EVEN BY AIR *(left)*.

club members met in Gerlach and journeyed together up the desert to the vicinity of the Little Joe Mine in the Calico Mountains. It was a sunny, pleasant day as the group set up camp, one member erecting a large tent fully equipped with cooking stove and spring beds. The rock hounds had started up the hillside to the gem-digging area when they saw a whirlwind headed for their camp. The tent was directly in its path and seconds later was sailing out over the playa disgorging its contents of stoves, beds, pots, and pans.

The camp was restored before nightfall, but the desert's weather was not finished with them. The

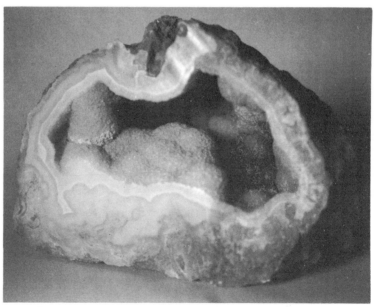

HALF OF GEODE FROM BLACK ROCK DESERT BASIN.

next morning they awakened to find four inches of wet snow covering the ground. The snow soon melted, but areas of the playa which had received runoff from the mountains gained axle-deep mud hidden beneath a deceptive dry layer, and on the way home all seven cars plowed into one of them.

After several hours of labor one car was extricated and dispatched to Gerlach for a tow truck. The rock hounds reached Reno the next morning in time to change clothes and get to their various jobs. Blue Monday was bluer than usual.

Because of their enjoyment of the desert and appreciation of its beauty, gem hunters are among the Black Rock's most environmentally concerned users. Organized gem and mineral clubs usually have strict codes of ethics which have been designed to protect the areas they visit. The use of four-wheel-drive vehicles is controlled to prevent ground cover and soil damage on hillsides, and when a group leaves a campsite it usually is cleaner than when they arrived.

Sometime ago the Reno Gem and Mineral Society had a Black Rock Desert cleanup trip. On the playa they formed search parties, each group combing a different section of the desert for litter.

James Allen Hardin would have liked those rock hounds.

NOTES TO CHAPTER VI

1. Dr. Vincent Gianella notes, "If the ore was 'carbonate of lead and silver' it would be impossible to melt it and form it into musket balls over a campfire with wood for fuel."

2. *The Eastern Slope* newspaper.

3. *Nevada Bureau of Mines Bulletin*, No. 59, shows that between 1875 and 1948 the Varyville district mines produced $108,477.

CHAPTER VII

The Ranchers

OVER MUCH of its vast expanse the playa is almost barren of plant life, a harsh environment for even its native animals. The surrounding upland areas, with additional moisture, provide grazing for cattle and sheep, and where mountain streams flow down canyons to the desert's edge, men have built ranches — some of which have existed for more than a century.*

For many years the Parman brothers were well-known, highly respected ranchers of northwestern Nevada. Their grandfather migrated to Surprise Valley on the California–Nevada border in 1873. His son George started in the sheep business in 1899 and during his life owned and sold a number of ranches in Surprise Valley and the surrounding country. In 1926 when the Miller and Lux properties were being liquidated, he and his four sons bought the Soldier Meadows Ranch. The youngest son, Ralph Parman, who now lives

---

Author's note: Very little has been written specifically on the ranching history of the Black Rock Desert basin. During 1974 and 1975 several ranchers of the area — men who had lived in the basin most or all of their lives — were interviewed, and most of the material in this chapter came from their memories. In instances where dates or other historical details were checked, their information was accurate.

The interviews produced approximately five hours of recorded conversation, only a small part of which was used in this book.

The tapes will be given to the University of Nevada, Reno Library, Special Collections, where they will be available to any serious researcher.

in Reno, spent most of his life on the Black Rock Desert ranches, and his knowledge of the region includes much early history passed on to him by older settlers.

The Soldier Meadows Ranch, which lies in a large canyon opening from the north out into the playa, was one of the early ranches. The military abandoned Fort McGary and Soldier Meadows in late 1868, and sometime afterward the two men who had operated the sutler's post at the fort acquired the meadows with the hope of making it into a ranch.[1] The military had leveled and plowed some of the area to grow hay for cavalry

THE DESERT BASIN'S UPLAND AREAS PROVIDE GRAZING FOR CATTLE AND SHEEP.

GEORGE PARMAN *(on right)* IN EARLY NINETEEN-TWENTIES.

horses, but the two new owners had little capital to purchase brood stock.

In the 1870s Dr. Hugh J. Glenn (after whom Glenn County, California, was named) expanded his cattle business into Oregon and Nevada by sending the legendary Pete French to Steen's Mountain in southern Oregon to build a ranch and a nephew named Crutcher to the Black Rock region where he obtained Soldier Meadows and eventually Paiute Meadows.

Ralph Parman remembers the story of Crutcher's acquisition of Paiute Meadows. A squatter, with a wife and son, had settled there hoping to build it into a paying ranch. The closest school was at Humboldt House (a settlement between Lovelock and Winnemucca); because be wished his boy to have an education, he decided to take his family there during the winter. He asked Crutcher to hold his land for him, and Crutcher agreed to do so.

When the squatter returned in the spring, Crutcher, backed by his crew of Spanish and Indian buckaroos, refused to return the property to him. The law was far away; the squatter moved on.

Instead of putting up hay for winter feeding, Crutcher annually moved his cattle down onto the north end of the desert where ryegrass and Indian ricegrass normally were plentiful. The winter of 1889-90 was exceptionally severe and disastrous to many Nevada and other western stockmen. With deep snow covering wild forage Crutcher had

THIS CABIN AT SUMMIT LAKE SUMMER SHEEP CAMP WAS BUILT
ABOUT 1884.

heavy losses, and eventually his holdings were sold to Miller and Lux.

Of all the great western cattle ranches, the Miller and Lux operation is probably the best known. The firm of Henry Miller and Charles Lux began in 1857 and grew into an empire of over 1,400,000 acres of patented land and many millions of acres of land on which it had grazing rights in California, Nevada, and Oregon. The tremendous area was required to support the firm's more than one million head of livestock.

Miller and Lux moved into the Black Rock basin in the 1880s, acquiring thousands of acres of rangeland which included the Leonard Creek and Quinn River Crossing ranches.

THE PARMAN BROTHERS, *(from left)*, LAWRENCE, VERN, HAROLD, AND RALPH.

Mitchell Bidart, one of the present owners of the Leonard Creek Ranch, points out that Miller and Lux, like Crutcher, did not put up hay for winter feeding of cattle. Enough hay was raised to take care of the horses, but the operation was based on the cattle foraging for themselves and an acceptance of large losses during severe winters. Throughout the year the cattle more or less ran free; they were rounded up only for branding and to be driven to market when four years old.

Ralph Parman tells of one winter when range conditions and lack of hay at the Paiute and Soldier Meadows ranches brought a decision to ship 800 head of cattle to Miller and Lux properties in California. The cattle were to be driven across the playa to the railroad at Sulphur to be loaded onto the Western Pacific.

The drive had progressed to somewhere near the center of the desert when a heavy fog enveloped the playa, producing conditions apparently similar to those faced by Fremont in January of 1844. The eight to ten buckaroos were experienced men but, unable to see any landmarks, became lost. It was impossible to hold the herd together, and the animals were abandoned with the hope they could be rounded up when the fog lifted.

Without a compass and able to see only a short distance in any direction, the men remained on the playa until the following day when they heard a train whistle and, with that as a guide, reached the railroad tracks, which they followed to Gerlach.

MILLER AND LUX FREIGHT TEAM, 1885.

Several days later most of the cattle were rounded up.

Henry Miller died in 1916. Without his driving energy his great ranching empire began to fade. It was liquidated in the 1920s.

Next to Miller and Lux, the Gerlach Land and Livestock Company was the largest early ranching operation in the Black Rock basin. In the 1890s Louis Gerlach, from the Stockton, California, area, bought the Deep Hole, Granite Creek, and Clear Creek ranches. Later his son, Fred, homesteaded the Fly Ranch. The Deep Hole Ranch (originally a station on the Nobles road, whose history included

Indian attacks) became the base of the company's extensive cattle operation in northern Nevada and bordering California.

Louis Gerlach was a shrewd businessman. Early in the 1900s he acquired the famous Bare ranch at the south end of Surprise Valley, increasing the company's holdings to what could be termed another ranching empire.

An interesting story about Mr. Gerlach is told by well-known Nevadan, Clarence J. Thornton, who as a youth worked on the Deep Hole Ranch. "I have heard many times, from people who should know, that when Louis Gerlach came to inspect the Deep Hole Ranch for the first time he was bitten by a tick. During that year there had been a number of cases of tick fever, so he was im-

Courtesy Humboldt County Library
MILLER LUX 1898, TWIN RIVER CROSSING.

DENIO WOOL FREIGHT TEAMS, 1885.

mediately taken by stage to a doctor in Reno. The doctor determined that the tick did not carry the disease, but Luis Gerlach never again set foot on the ranch. All future business with his superintendent, Jim Raser, was conducted in Reno."

The Gerlach Land and Livestock Company suffered the fate of Miller and Lux and many of the other great ranches. Louis Gerlach, the builder, reached an age at which he could no longer manage his complex, widely spread operation. His son Fred took over the responsibility for a number of years until the property was leased and, in the 1940s, sold to individual ranchers. Anyone visiting the Deep Hole Ranch today would find it difficult to believe that it once put up 400 tons of hay annually and was the center of the activity required to manage thousands of cattle and the vast range-

land on which they lived. The main ranch house
and other buildings have been burned to the
ground. Oddly enough, the original Nobles road
station still stands.

The Fisk Ranch, which has remained in the
ownership of the family which first homesteaded
it, lies along the highway between Gerlach and
Surprise Valley. William Fisk, born in 1869,
worked for Miller and Lux as a young man and
later for the Western Pacific Railroad during its
construction through the Black Rock basin. In
1911 the Fisks homesteaded 160 acres in a corner
of the basin called Squaw Valley. Since then the
ranch has grown to 1,582 acres and is currently
operated by William Fisk's son Clyde and grandson Bill Fisk.

Clyde Fisk tells of the time a neighbor thought

DEEP HOLE RANCH, 1890s.

Courtesy Nevada Historical Society

DEEP HOLE RANCH, 1890s.

Courtesy Robert Amesbury

ONLY A FEW CHARRED BOARDS OF LOUIS GERLACH'S RANCH
HOUSE REMAIN, BUT THE ORIGINAL DEEP HOLE STATION,
BUILT OF ROCKS IN THE MID 1850s, STILL STANDS *(left)*.
Deep Hole Spring is in foreground.

he had good reason to have a thick-walled house. The Indian wars had ended long before 1911 when a small band of Indian men and women led by "Shoshoni Mike" killed four ranchers in Little High Rock Canyon.[2] Attempting to elude a posse, the Indian band crossed the Black Rock Desert in midwinter and headed east. They were overtaken north of Golconda, Nevada, and during the engagement which followed one member of the posse and all the Indians except a woman and three children were killed.

After so many years of peace the event was a shock to many Nevadans living in the northern part of the state, and when it was followed by false rumors of Indian war parties seeking revenge at least one Black Rock rancher was persuaded to reinforce the walls of his house with foot-thick juniper posts, creating a miniature fort.

The history of the Leonard Creek Ranch extends back at least into the 1860s. In 1865 the stream itself may have been called Fish Creek and later changed to Leonard Creek when a man of that name settled beside it. Little is known about Mr. Leonard.

In the 1870s the ranch was owned by a man named Derby. In addition to a cattle operation, Mr. Derby bred and raised racehorses. The outline of his racetrack can still be seen.

The heavy winter of 1879-80 depleted Derby's cattle herds, and in the mid-eighties the ranch was sold to Miller and Lux. In 1926, during the liquidation of Henry Miller's great spread, two Basque ranchers, Michel Bidart and Ramon Montero, bought the Leonard Creek property; their sons, Mitchell Bidart and Lawrence Montero, operate it today.

Generally considered cattle country, the Black Rock basin and surrounding mountains were once heavily used as sheep ranges. Ralph Parman discussed his knowledge of the history of that period and his participation in the sheep industry:

"Although in the 1870s and 80s one of the routes over which California sheep were trailed to markets in the intermountain region passed across parts of the Black Rock basin, as far as I know the first sheepman to use the area annually as either a winter or summer range was John O'Kane who operated a hay ranch near Lovelock, Nevada. Beginning in about 1883 he summered sheep in the Donnelly Mountain and Summit Lake area and wintered them on hay and ranges near Lovelock.

"In 1903 Carl Wheeler, son of Daniel C. Wheeler,[3] bought O'Kane's sheep and his deeded land and range rights in the basin. In 1907 Carl Wheeler sold the entire outfit to his younger brother, Don, who operated it until 1922,[4] the year that he died from exposure when his car became mired in mud while crossing the desert on a winter night.

"In 1927 my brothers and I acquired the Wheeler Ranch and, in partnership with Louis Valardi, ran about 13,000 sheep. We wintered the bands on each side of the desert in the low foothills of the Black Rock Range and the Calico

Mountains. We lambed on the range starting about the fifth of April and sheared about the middle of May.

"Gradually working to higher elevations, the bands were held on the intermediate ranges until about the first of July and then pushed up onto the high summer range. In October we would make up winter bands of 2,000 to 2,500 head and graze downward, staying ahead of the heavy snowfall, until we were again near the desert.

"In addition to this type of operation, sheep were trailed into the basin's winter ranges from ranches such as the Fee outfit near Fort Bidwell in Surprise Valley, California. The Fee family were among the earliest settlers in Surprise Valley, and, although brothers Ernest and Charles Fee were cattlemen, in about 1920 they joined with two other men to buy a sheep outfit. Their operation was based on trailing their bands to the foothill region on the southeast side of the Black Rock playa in the fall and returning to the northeastern California summer ranges in the spring.

"In the 1930s, after the passage of the Taylor Grazing Act, Laurance J. Fee, son of Ernest Fee, sold the sheep. Today his Fee Ranch, Inc. properties, which extend into Nevada, are devoted to cattle raising.

"In the early years there were many tramp sheepmen who owned no base ranch or property and paid no taxes unless a county assessor caught up with them — which was unlikely. Unlike the legitimate operators, most of them had little interest in range management or private property

CRAIG OBTAINED THE ADVICE OF MEMBERS OF TWO PROMI-
NENT BASQUE SHEEP RANCHING FAMILIES IN ATTEMPTING TO
MAKE THIS PAINTING OF A TYPICAL SHEEPHERDER'S CAMP AC-
CURATE IN EVEN SMALL DETAILS.

boundaries, and they probably did considerable
damage to the basin.

"Eventually the state legislature passed laws to
protect landowners by giving them the authority
to file trespass suits.

"Sheep operations have been often blamed for
most of the overgrazing which has occurred in the
basin, but from my observations the blame should
be divided among the three types of livestock —
sheep, cattle, and horses. One of our largest problems was the range horses which were branded,
owned, and claimed. They were rounded up at

least once a year for branding and so forth, but aside from that they remained on the range throughout the year in numbers far in excess of local needs. When the Miller and Lux outfit was liquidated, over 800 horses were taken from the Soldier Meadows area."

What was it like to ranch in the Black Rock Desert basin?

When they operated the Soldier Meadows and Wheeler[5] ranches, the Parmans owned 14,000 acres of patented land and had grazing rights on more than 380,000 acres. Along with many other ranchers, they were hard hit by the depression in the early 1930s. Ralph explains, "We were forced into liquidation but were able to pay all of our debts, and in 1937 Verne and I bought back the Wheeler Ranch and operated it for another twenty-one years.

"Ranching was hard work for the whole family; my sisters even worked in the hayfields. During some winters it got to over twenty degrees below zero, and that's when you have to be out handling stock. We had some rough times, but we had a lot of good times too."

Mitchell Bidart briefly explained the operations of the Leonard Creek Ranch. "We have more conveniences now, like electricity and a telephone, but some things haven't changed very much. Some people probably think machines have replaced horses. We use horses. Sometimes we load them in a truck and take them to the end of the road, but from there on it's about the same as it was a

SUMMER SHEEP CAMP ON SUMMIT LAKE MOUNTAIN.

hundred years ago. Without horses we couldn't handle cattle in the type of rangeland which covers most of northern Nevada.

"We grow hay for winter feeding, but, like most Great Basin ranchers, we depend primarily on the range. It has been claimed that the big herds of the early days, like those of Miller and Lux, destroyed a lot of the range. Probably there was damage from overstocking, especially during the dry years, but now when we get enough rain and snow in the winter the grasses come back. Moisture is the important thing.

"Years ago we had Indians from the Summit Lake area working for us. They were good workers, conscientious. As kids we were raised with them."

Mr. Louis E. Lay, whose family ranched along the eastern edge of the basin and the Jackson range, tells how children of that area were provided with an equal opportunity for education. A

CORRAL AT LEONARD CREEK RANCH. HORSES ARE A NECESSITY IN HANDLING CATTLE IN THE TYPE OF RANGELAND WHICH COVERS MUCH OF NORTHERN NEVADA.

Courtesy Mrs. Vern Parman
CHARLIE AND HATTIE GOING HOME FROM A SUNDAY VISIT
WHEN BOTH OF THEM WERE OVER NINETY YEARS OF AGE.
They were friends of Mrs. Vern Parman when she was a child and taught
her to braid rawhide and hair ropes.

schoolhouse was built on a site which was about the same distance from each of the ranches which had children of school age. When graduation changed the situation, the equal distance balance was re-established by loading the little school house on a hay wagon and moving it to a new central location.

If you had it to do over again?

Vern Parman died in February of 1974. His widow, Ruth, who now lives in Reno remembers, "Those were hard but happy times — every day was different. And there was something unusual about the desert. We didn't have a church building, but you could feel a higher power all around you. All the families that we knew out there felt the same way. If I had it to do over again I wouldn't want to change anything."

The Parman brothers sold the ranch in 1958. Ralph explains, "Prices for ranch products were low, and it was difficult to hire competent help because the wages were higher in the cities.

"But I guess the real reason we left the desert was that we were getting along in years. If we had been younger, we'd probably still be out there."

Mitchell Bidart pointed out, "When you're born in this kind of environment, I guess it's in your blood. We go on vacations to see other places, but even then I like to go to another desert like in Arizona. The ranch has been a big part of our lives, and we've enjoyed it.

"Sometimes people come out here and say this is the kind of life they'd like to live — no pressures. Well, we have pressures, all ranchers do, but still it is a quieter life.

"We also have people come to the ranch and ask, 'How do you live out here? I don't see how anything could survive.'

"But they don't understand the desert; they don't know how much it does produce, how much life there is. You have to live in the desert to see this."

NOTES TO CHAPTER VII

1. Ralph Parman believes the sutlers' names were Crocker and Clark.

2. There are several books written about this event: Effie Mona Mack, *The Indian Massacre of 1911 at Little High Rock Canyon, Nevada* (Sparks, Nevada: Western Printing and Publishing Co., 1968); K. D. Scott, *Frozen Grass* (Tahlequal, Oklahoma: Pan Press, 1964); D. O. Hyde, *The Last Free Man* (New York: Dial Press, 1973).

3. Daniel C. Wheeler (not a relative of author) was one of Nevada's best known and most successful early sheep ranchers. His base ranch was several miles south of Reno.

4. Nevada State Division of Vital Statistics.

5. The Wheeler Ranch (also known as the Donnelly Ranch or Parman Ranch) is located on Donnelly Creek, where Goldsborough Bruff and other 1849 emigrants stopped to rest.

CHAPTER VIII

The Desert Today

AT FIRST it was difficult to believe the newspaper article. But it was true; the Black Rock-Smoke Creek Desert was being considered as a disposal site for San Francisco's garbage and trash.

A great desert playa, equal in its strange beauty to the more famous Death Valley and of greater historical significance, was to become a giant garbage dump.

To those who knew this lonely section of our earth it was incredible.

Not many years ago those who enjoyed the desert believed it would remain primitive and undisturbed because no one else wanted it. Man, with his sewage and other urban problems, was currently moving into the Sierra Nevada; highways, with their noise and confusion, had stretched great bands of asphalt across desert valleys and cut deep gashes into the mountains which blocked their way. But most of the big playa remained tranquil and lonely, and the people who used it thought it would stay that way because it had nothing to offer those men whose only goal is something they call progress.

Almost since the first white man came to it, the desert has had to survive minor threats to its

Courtesy Mrs. Vern Parman

TOWN OF GERLACH PROBABLY IN MID-1920s.

WELL KNOWN BUSINESSMAN BRUNO SELMI ON GERLACH'S
MAIN STREET TODAY.

beauty. By the end of 1849 the playa was cluttered with dead livestock and abandoned wagons. Hardin City, the ranchers, and the railroad made changes. Even the navy used it for many years as an air-to-air target range. The towns of Gerlach and Empire came into being, and a rock and dirt fill across the playa between them allowed State Highway 34 to continue north. Dirt and gravel roads surround the entire playa, and during the dry season ranchers and visitors use shortcut trails across the lake bed.

But despite these disturbances, the desert has retained its primitive character. The Western Pacific Railroad, following a general route first explored by Lieutenant E. G. Beckwith in 1854, laid its tracks largely above the south and east edges of the playa where they are scarcely noticeable. Empire and Gerlach, built within a few miles of each other, affect a relatively small area. Empire is a mining community, while Gerlach (originally built to service the railroad) is a necessary crossroad town providing ranchers and travelers with food, lodging, gasoline, and other necessities. It is a picturesque little community, resembling a motion-picture version of the Old West.[1]

Dirt and graveled roads have little effect on the scenery because of the camouflage of sagebrush along their sides. Vehicle tracks across the playa, which through long use have worn down into the lake bed, seem a natural part of the desert, like the old trails made by Indians or the ruts of forty-niners wagons.

For more than a century the desert had existed

in a fair state of harmony with the white man before someone devised a plan which would effectively and permanently destroy the great playa's esthetic values. In July of 1967 Reno newspapers revealed the possibility that a project was being formulated to bury San Francisco's garbage in the Black Rock-Smoke Creek Desert. Approximately 1,500 tons of the material would be transported there daily by the Western Pacific Railroad.

The rumor quickly brought strong reactions from some northern Nevadans — those who resented California garbage going to any Nevada area and those concerned about the desert. But before it was necessary for Nevada officials to consider any proposal, the dumping site was switched to an area east of the Sierra Army Depot at Herlong, California, and later to a site closer to the bay city.

In a way the proposal was beneficial — it was a warning that the desert's future was not secure.

The nation's current search for additional energy could affect the Black Rock Desert. Hot springs scattered throughout the basin have attracted the attention of agencies and individuals attempting to find geothermal energy sites. The temperature, quantity, and dissolved minerals of the water are some of the factors which decide whether, under present technology, a site is practicable; to determine these requisites, underground drilling is usually necessary.

If, in the opinion of thoroughly competent authorities, underground exploration is warranted, there is little doubt that it will take place. But many people hope that damage to historical and scenic areas will be minimized by limiting installation locations and types of construction. Considering scientific and technological achievements, it should be possible to tap and use geothermal energy with little destruction or alteration of the surrounding environment.

One of the strongest fears of those who would preserve the desert concerns the possible construction of modern access roads extending onto the playa for geothermal exploration or other purposes. Current playa roads are worn down below the surface of the lake bed so that from a hundred yards or so they are usually invisible. But a road which could be traveled during wet weather would have to be constructed on a rock and dirt fill, which in most areas of the desert would destroy the playa's scenic values.

There is another strong fear, a common one throughout the West, concerned with the unscrupulous promoter-speculator who obtains land through lease or purchase and manipulates financial gain with no thought for the damaged environment or injured people he leaves behind. Maybe the desert's most vital need is protection from those who believe deserts are worthless wastelands unless they can be developed into something having commercial value.

With the exception of a few small areas, the Black Rock Desert belongs to all of us, whether we live in the West or the East. It is public land managed for us by the Bureau of Land Management of the Department of the Interior. Management

A THUNDERHEAD BUILDING OVER THE DESERT.

plans are formulated by BLM personnel and presented for public consideration before they are formally adopted. The open meetings offer all interested citizens an opportunity to participate in the planning.

Current personnel of the Bureau of Land Management in Nevada undoubtedly recognize the recreational values of the Black Rock Desert. Chester E. Conrad, manager of the Winnemucca District, wrote in part, "Our Recreation Information System has identified the Black Rock Desert as having high recreational values in the following recreation opportunities: 1. Sightseeing. . . . , 2.

TODAY, MORE THAN 127 YEARS AFTER BRUFF, MANY PEOPLE VISIT THE HOT SPRINGS AT THE BLACK ROCK.
Temperatures at Black Rock Spring, Double Hot Spring and Great Boiling Spring (ranging from 80° to 90°C or 176° to 194°F) make them dangerous to children who might fall into the near-boiling water.

Collecting, Mineral, 3. Specialized Activities. . . . ,
4. Primitive Values.

"It is an extremely unique area and setting. Few
locations within our district will rate as high in as
many recreational opportunities as the Black Rock
Desert and surrounding peaks. It will be identified
in the planning process as a sensitive recreation
area recommended for protection of the above
values."[2]

Leonard Creek rancher Mitchell Bidart commented on present use of the desert, "Most people
who go out there really like the desert, and they
take good care of it. You don't see the trash that
you do at some of the other recreation areas."

The desert probably has remained clean because
it does not provide a type of recreation which at-
tracts the "outdoor slob." Almost all Black Rock
visitors are interested in history, scenery, rocks or
just solitude.

Most people who enjoy desert country are experienced in living in an arid outdoor environment. However, first-time visitors to the Black
Rock probably should be aware of several conditions somewhat peculiar to this playa.

Over the years many people have become lost or
had their cars break down or become mired in
mud on the Black Rock Desert. Stranded far out
on the Playa in hot or extremely cold temperatures can be serious, and a first-time expedition on
the lake bed should be made with a companion
who knows the desert and its pitfalls. Also, there is

no better safety factor than traveling in a party of two or more vehicles.

Playa roads should not be used during winter or early spring without reliable information on their condition, and even during the dry season a weather eye should be kept on clouds which appear to be building into thunderheads. A thunderstorm on the desert is a spectacular sight, with wind pushing a wall of dust across the playa ahead of solid sheets of rain and with lightning slashing down from black clouds. But in minutes the lake bed can become so slippery most cars are unable to maintain traction.

Regardless of weather conditions, there are places on the desert where it is never entirely safe

A DESERT CAMP WITH JACKSON MOUNTAINS IN BACKGROUND.

RAIN CLOUDS WARN THAT IT IS TIME TO LEAVE THE PLAYA.

to drive. Over the years many automobiles have become mired in the bed of the Quinn (Queen's) River, where a hard, dry surface layer often covers deep mud. Some of the drivers and passengers of stuck cars have walked more than thirty miles to Gerlach, while others have headed for the Western Pacific Railroad tracks where engineers have stopped their trains to pick them up. The sink of the Quinn River, which covers a large area south of the Black Rock Range, can be muddy when most of the playa is dry.

Although it may seem unlikely that people returning from a hike across the relatively flat playa would have difficulty finding their cars, it does occur quite often, especially when an automobile's color is light enough to blend with the alkali flat. Parking on an elevated area with a brightly colored flag tied to the radio antenna may save a nerve-wracking and embarrasing experience.

When traveling into isolated areas of the desert, the condition of the automobile is especially important. Tires, fan belt, radiator hoses, and fuel pumps are parts which often cause trouble. Extra engine oil, ample drinking water plus enough water to at least refill the car's radiator, a heavy jack, several wood blocks, a set of tools, and a shovel are probably minimum requirements.

A desert is not the deadly dangerous environment it is so often pictured to be. From many areas of the Black Rock playa it is possible to see at least one patch of trees on the edge of the lake bed, and trees almost always mean a ranch.

Panic, which overcomes sensible thinking, is the greatest hazard facing a lost or stranded person. Man is capable of solving most survival problems if he maintains his ability to think.

Over the years the Black Rock playa has been relatively kind to its visitors.

Although most of the desert is visible from the high roads cut into the hillsides above the lake bed, the unusual scenery of a large playa cannot be fully realized if viewed only from its edge. Many ancient lake beds are not suitable for automobile travel; their surfaces are too rough, too wet, or too sandy, and construction of modern roads on them would diminish their most unique qualities. Nature made the Black Rock Desert's beauty available.

Approximately three miles northeast of Gerlach on State Highway 34 a dirt road turns off to drop down onto the playa and branch into three main routes. In general, the set of tracks which bear farthest to the right crosses the playa to a ranch. The road on the left, deeply worn into the lake bed, provides a fast, dry-weather alternate for a short section of State Highway 34 and for a long stretch of the high road to Soldier Meadows. Branches from this left-hand desert road also lead to the Black Rock and Double Hot Springs. The location of the third route, a shortcut to Sulphur, is more difficult to describe — emphasizing the advisability of making the first playa trip with someone who knows the desert.

Probably most first-time visitors with an interest in Western history wish to see the famous Black Rock hill which is almost thirty airline miles northeast of Gerlach. Following the left-hand road, the desert is smooth, and driving a car across it seems almost like riding in a boat on a calm lake. From its edges the playa is a barren, white flat; but as one moves out onto it, it comes to life — begins to stretch into a spectacular landscape. The rugged beauty of the bordering mountains is emphasized by the flatness of the lake bed, and ahead the desert dissolves in the distance.

Speeding toward the northeast, a "rooster-tail" of dust boiling up behind the car, a hill of dark rock comes into sight. It is still far away, but it sharply stands out against its background. Although you have not seen it before, you immediately know what it is.

Gazing at it across the playa you understand why the Applegates, Peter Lassen, and thousands of emigrants used it as a landmark.

There are many reasons why people go to the desert, some of which are not easily explained. Kenneth J. Carpenter, University of Nevada special collections librarian, spends many weekends in the Black Rock basin. I asked him why, and he answered, "Your request seems simple to comply with — but it isn't. As you know, I go to the Black Rock alone, with neither companion nor dog. Some think I am foolish doing this, but I know the country so well and its attraction is so strong that I never feel alone or afraid (even last spring when I got badly stuck). I have been many places in the world, many places of primitive beauty. I grew up in Yosemite and when a youngster roamed the Sierra alone summer after summer. So I am used to the outdoors and to being alone. Man is a social animal. I recognize this and could never be a true hermit. But today others are too much with us and the petty (sometimes great) worries that beset us cannot be alleviated in a crowd — at least for me they can't. But nowhere have I felt serenity and welcome solitude more strongly than on the Black Rock Desert. I sit alone in the evening looking out over the desert and feel layers of tension and worry washing away. A few years ago my former secretary said to me one morning: 'You've been out on the desert.' I asked her how she knew and

Courtesy Dr. Walter Orr Roberts

THE BLACK ROCK PHOTOGRAPHED FROM LOW FLYING AIRCRAFT.

she replied, 'I can always tell, for your face is so calm when you get back.' "

To those who love the desert, its beauty and primitive qualities are unique and precious. To them it is a world of stillness, of vast space, of great mountains with canyons so sharp and deep that the sun's rays hardly touch their floors. It is a region of brightness where rocks and plants, scrubbed by windblown sand, sparkle with their cleanliness. It is a land of mystery where ancient man left evidence of his visits thousands of years ago. It is a place of history where Indian warriors fought for their way of life and where legends of the Old West were born.

During its hours of sunlight the great playa is bright and friendly; but when evening cools its surface and late shadows sharpen the walls of mountain canyons, it becomes an enchanted place where one can visualize weary emigrants crossing the broad flat or watch a fierce raider on a white horse lead his band toward Paiute Creek.

And, later, when light from a billion stars gives the desert an eerie quality, there are those who might hear an ancient Indian's silent plea, "When it was ours it was a sacred place. Now that it is yours, preserve its dignity and beauty — treat it with respect."

NOTES TO CHAPTER VIII

1. In 1926 the desert had a genuine motion-picture town. Samuel Goldwyn built it for the filming of Harold Bell Wright's *The Winning of Barbara Worth*, which starred Vilma Banky and Gary Moore. Clarence Thorton remembers the make-believe town and how it was flattened several times by the high winds of the desert's thunderstorms. Small pieces of weathered wood, scattered over several acres of the playa, still mark the site.

2. Conard to author, 3 November 1975.

Appendix

(This appendix has been added to update the earlier print-
ings of THE BLACK ROCK DESERT, especially in regard to
recent paleontological discoveries on the Desert.)

Update — Chapter One "Before It Was Desert"

Modern Man constantly searches for knowledge
of the past, possibly hoping it will help him to better
understand the present. The date Early Man first
came to North America and his ways of living in the
environment he found there have been of special
interest; and, since the last printing of this book,
there have been discoveries which offer hope of
additional information — information recorded
thousands of years ago in the lake bed sediments
of the Black Rock Desert.

On Labor Day, 1979, Steve Wallmann, a logger
from Grants Pass, Oregon, was roaming the playa
near an ancient Lake Lahontan shoreline when he
noticed a light colored object surrounded by bone
fragments. Years before he had seen a mammoth
tooth in a museum, and when he kneeled beside
the object, he thought he recognized a similarity.

Believing the site might be of some value to science, he left it undisturbed and, during the following winter, contacted archeologist Dr. C. William
Clewlow of the University of California at Los
Angeles. Dr. Clewlow had spent several summers
studying the surface archeology of the Black Rock
Desert and, because of the types of artifacts he
found, he often had been nagged with the feeling

WILLIAM A. MOORE PAINTING, FROM PERMANENT COLLECTION OF FAVELL MUSEUM OF ARTS AND ARTIFACTS, KLAMATH FALLS, OREGON. MR. MOORE, WHO PARTICIPATED IN THE 1982 MAMMOTH EXCAVATION, USED HIS ARTIST'S LICENSE TO DEPICT THE BACKGROUND SOMEWHAT AS IT IS TODAY.

that the wind eroded playa contained additional knowledge of Early Man.

In the summer of 1980, Wallmann guided Clewlow to the site, and paleontologist Richard Reynolds, of the Page Museum at the LaBrea Tar Pits in Los Angeles, identified the object as the third molar of a mammoth. It was when a closer inspection of the area revealed the eroded ends of two tusks, indicating that more of the animal lay below the surface, that Dr. Clewlow's interest soared beyond the value of the mammoth itself to the possibility that it might provide evidence of a connection with Pleistocene man.